D1453873

Aidan Nichols, O. P.

Chalice of God

A Systematic Theology in Outline

LITURGICAL PRESS
Collegeville, Minnesota

www.litpress.org

1   2   3   4   5   6   7   8   9

Library of Congress Cataloging-in-Publication Data

Nichols, Aidan.
    Chalice of God : a systematic theology in outline / Aidan Nichols.
        p.   cm.
    Includes bibliographical references (p.   ).
    ISBN 978-0-8146-3431-8 — ISBN 978-0-8146-3432-5 (e-book)
    1. Catholic Church—Doctrines.   2. Theology, Doctrinal.   I. Title.
  BX1751.3.N53   2012
  230'.2—dc23   2012003900

For Christians believed not only that the temporal world was an expression of God's will and wisdom—in something like the way that pagans had believed that it was ruled and shaped by the gods, or that it was a shadow of the world of the Ideas—but that God had entered into that world, using its analogous resemblance to him in order to form it into a vessel for his actual presence.

S. Caldecott, *Beauty for Truth's Sake*

Contents

Preface

I am using this preface to explain to the reader why this book has the unusual format that it does.

The first thing that will strike him or her is that the first person singular occurs more than is customary in a theological work. This is because, as the introduction will start by saying, this text is meant to be something of a manifesto, where my own personal convictions about how best to proceed in expounding theology are aired. I hope it is not too much to claim for it the status of a fresh approach to the Catholic understanding of the world and human existence in revelation's light. To see just what this "fresh approach" amounts to, readers will have to read the book. And, since it is a kind of manifesto, this need not take them too long. In any case, the epigram from the writings of Stratford Caldecott which precedes this preface will give them a taster.

It is because the book is in the nature of a personal declaration that I include a list of my published writings hitherto. I have not put that in so as to give myself a pat on the back. Rather, the list is there for two reasons. The first is straightforward: it is to show that plenty of solid reading and writing has gone on in my life before I've ventured to present anything as adventurous as a theological manifesto.

The other reason is more subtle: I think my attraction to a particular set of theological writers, or my approach to theological topics I've considered in the past, was guided by an implicit sense of the theological vision I have here articulated in concise form.

Then there is something else the reader will pick up. After the introduction, this book does not consist of continuous prose. Rather, each chapter is made up of distinct theses separated from each other by numbers. This has two explanations, one theoretical and the other practical. The theoretical explanation is that there may well be people who do not want to "buy into" the whole package I am offering, but who nevertheless would like to take away from it particular parts to be used again elsewhere, fitted into other patterns of thinking. The practical explanation is that the distinct theses could well serve as starting points for discussion in, for example, classes for students of theology in universities or seminaries or even online.

The next peculiarity is that particular theses are frequently punctuated by cross-references to other theses in the book, whether these have preceded or are going to come after. This is not relevant to the manifesto form so much as to the other category in which a librarian might choose to catalogue this book—namely, as a short systematics. The whole point of a systematics, as distinct from a dogmatics or what I have elsewhere called a "theological introduction to Catholicism," is that everything is quite consciously made to interlock with everything else. The whole thing is organic, or, to change the metaphor, it moves in a circle. The cross-references will, I hope, help the reader to check this out.

Finally, there are a number of images drawn from Byzantine and Russian art. They are included for their own beauty as Christian artworks. But this precisely means these images are there as an inspiration to readers, to let minds and hearts travel up toward the mysteries of which I have written inadequately and yet as well as I could.

Acknowledgments

Permissions have been requested to reprint the following: Intercultura for permission to reproduce the cover image and plate 2; Iskusstvo-XXI Vek for permission to reproduce plates 1, 3, and 6; St. Vladimir's Seminary Press for permission to reproduce plate 4; Skira Editore for permission to reproduce plate 5; and Br. Oliver Keenan, O. P., for his photographic skills in incorporating these images into the text of the book.

At the time of publication, these permissions were still in process. We welcome any aid in securing the permissions for these images.

Other Works by Aidan Nichols

Foundations of the Faith

Theology of Revelation

The Art of God Incarnate: Theology and Image in Christian Tradition (London: Darton, Longman and Todd, 1980)

Lovely, Like Jerusalem: The Fulfillment of the Old Testament in Christ and the Church (San Francisco: Ignatius Press, 2007)

Philosophy of Religion

A Grammar of Consent: The Existence of God in Christian Tradition (Notre Dame, IN: University of Notre Dame Press, 1991)

Theological Catechetics

The Splendour of Doctrine: The Catechism of the Catholic Church *on Christian Believing* (Edinburgh: T. and T. Clark, 1995)

The Service of Glory: The Catechism of the Catholic Church *on Worship, Ethics, Spirituality* (Edinburgh: T. and T. Clark, 1997)

Come to the Father: An Invitation to Share the Faith of the Catholic Church (London: St. Paul's Publishing, 2000)

Ecclesial Dogmatics

Epiphany: A Theological Introduction to Catholicism (Collegeville, MN: Liturgical Press, 1996)

Theological Method

The Shape of Catholic Theology: An Introduction to Its Sources, Principles and History (Collegeville, MN: Liturgical Press, 1991)

Apologetics

Criticising the Critics: Catholic Apologias for Today (Oxford: Family Publications, 2010)

Theological *Ressourcement*

Ancients

Byzantine Gospel: Maximus the Confessor in Modern Scholarship (Edinburgh: T. and T. Clark, 1993)

Discovering Aquinas: An Introduction to His Life, Work and Influence (London: Darton, Longman and Todd, 2002)

Moderns

The Theology of Joseph Ratzinger: An Introductory Study (Edinburgh: T. and T. Clark, 1988; re-printed as *The Thought of Pope Benedict XVI*, London: Continuum, 2005; 2nd edition, London: Continuum, 2007)

Yves Congar (London: Geoffrey Chapman, 1989)

From Newman to Congar: The Idea of Doctrinal Development from the Victorians to the Second Vatican Council (Edinburgh: T. and T. Clark, 1990)

Dominican Gallery: Portrait of a Culture (Leominster: Gracewing, 1997)

Catholic Thought Since the Enlightenment: A Survey (Leominster: Gracewing, 1998)

The Word Has Been Abroad: A Guide through Balthasar's Aesthetics (Edinburgh: T. and T. Clark, 1998)

No Bloodless Myth: A Guide through Balthasar's Dramatics (Edinburgh: T. and T. Clark, 2000)

Say It Is Pentecost: A Guide through Balthasar's Logic (Edinburgh: T. and T. Clark, 2001)

A Spirituality for the Twenty-First Century (Huntington, IN: Our Sunday Visitor, 2003)

Scattering the Seed. A Guide through Balthasar's Early Writings on Philosophy and the Arts (London: Continuum, 2006)

Divine Fruitfulness: A Guide through Balthasar's Writings beyond the Trilogy (London: Continuum, 2007)

Reason with Piety: Garrigou-Lagrange in the Service of Catholic Thought (Naples, FL: Sapientia Press, 2008)

From Hermes to Benedict XVI: Faith and Reason in Modern Catholic Thought (Leominster: Gracewing, 2009)

Romance and System: The Theological Synthesis of Matthias Joseph Scheeben (Denver, CO: Augustine Institute Press, Nova et Vetera Book Series, 2010)

A Key to Balthasar: Hans Urs von Balthasar on Beauty, Goodness, and Truth (London: Darton, Longman and Todd, 2011)

Cult and Culture

Holy Order: The Apostolic Ministry from the New Testament to the Second Vatican Council (Dublin: Veritas, 1990)

The Holy Eucharist: From the New Testament to Pope John Paul II (Dublin: Veritas, 1991)

Looking at the Liturgy: A Critical View of Its Contemporary Form (San Francisco: Ignatius Press, 1996)

Christendom Awake: On Reenergizing the Church in Culture (Edinburgh: T. and T. Clark, 1999)

Scribe of the Kingdom: Essays on Theology and Culture. 2 vols. (London: Sheed and Ward, 1994)

Beyond the Blue Glass: Catholic Essays on Faith and Culture. 2 vols. (London: Saint Austin Press, 2002)

Hopkins: Theologian's Poet; An Introduction and a Commentary on Selected Poems (Ann Arbor, MI: Sapientia Press, 2006)

Redeeming Beauty: Essays on Sacral Aesthetics (Burlington, VT: Ashgate, 2007)

The Realm: An Unfashionable Essay on the Conversion of England (Oxford: Family Publications, 2008)

G. K. Chesterton, Theologian (Manchester, NH: Sophia Institute Press, 2009)

The Poet as Believer: A Theological Study of Paul Claudel (Burlington, VT: Ashgate, 2011)

The Latin Clerk: The Life, Work, and Travels of Adrian Fortescue (Cambridge: Lutterworth, 2011)

Lost in Wonder: Essays on Liturgy and the Arts (Burlington, VT: Ashgate, 2011)

Ecumenical Evaluation

Theology in the Russian Diaspora: Church, Fathers, Eucharist in Nikolai Afanas´ev, 1893–1966 (Cambridge: Cambridge University Press, 1989)

Rome and the Eastern Churches: A Study in Schism (Edinburgh: T. and T. Clark, 1991; 2nd edition, San Francisco: Ignatius Press, 2010)

The Panther and the Hind: A Theological History of Anglicanism (Edinburgh: T. and T. Clark, 1992)

Light from the East: Authors and Themes in Orthodox Theology (London: Sheed and Ward, 1995)

Wisdom from Above: A Primer in the Theology of Father Sergei Bulgakov (Leominster: Gracewing, 2005)

Introduction

Chalice of God aims to be a work of Catholic systematics. It is also something of a manifesto for the theological scene. I claim it to be innovatory not in its doctrinal content (I am, I trust, fully orthodox) but in its organization, as indicated by its governing metaphor—the "chalice" of the world, filled by the libation of God. The building blocks I have used are no doubt in place in a variety of other writers (I give some references in the text and its endnotes), but the way I have put them together in the architecture of this systematics is my own.

My fundamental commitment is to high mediaeval scholasticism and the mid-twentieth-century movement of *ressourcement* which accessed ancient springs: the holistic reading of Scripture typical of the best patristic exegesis, the fathers themselves, the liturgies and iconography of Tradition. In that latter respect, I am Byzantinising, though I by no means discount the Roman liturgy and the resources of Western Christian art. I do not consider the scholastic dimension to be in competition with the Greek East: the Byzantines too had their schoolmen who studied with Aristotle as well as Plato. My masters are St. Thomas in his relation to the fathers and Hans Urs von Balthasar in his relation to both at once.

While I find merit in romanticism, and therefore in the tradition of German thought that is its backcloth, I have no wish to be thought modern, recalling the regrettable commonality that joins together the *via moderna* of late mediaeval philosophy and twentieth-century cultural modernity. Both the nominalist and *homo modernus* live in a world that lacks the presupposition of ontological order. They thus find themselves confronted by an array of merely individual facts, to be discovered empirically and used pragmatically. Reason gets reduced to the dimensions of an instrument (its primary expression will be technology and its achievements) rather than recognized in the ampler way truly *philosophical* reason deserves—a way of wisdom about the world and human existence.

Nor do I have hankerings after association with postmodernism, whose therapy for the condition of modernity—the shaking of all identity in the name of endless decentering—exacerbates the disease it would cure. On the contrary, I gladly embrace metanarrative; I find the ability to tell the story of one's life the chief symptom of selfhood, and I take the biblical narrative, read realistically, to signal the advent of consummatory divine interaction with human beings. Likewise, far from deploring it, I affirm "logocentrism," for the Word has guaranteed words, not least those of his holy prophets and apostles. Through the gift of language he has secured not only the reference and meaning speakers characteristically intend, fortified in the hagiographs by the charism of inspiration, but also the capacity of inscribed words cumulatively to deploy their own virtualities, which, for Scripture, culminates via a homogeneous process of interpretation in a Christological understanding of the biblical canon as a whole. I certainly do not flinch from the idea of totality (yet another bugbear of postmoderns), since revelation constitutes a *totum* greater than which none can be conceived, able as it is to accommodate all elements of truth and goodness within itself. And finally, I am not fearful of the notion of unity, since I place my enterprise under the auspices of the *one*, holy, catholic, and apostolic Church. In fact I accept the "scandal" (the claim is a stumbling block for many) whereby the mysteric Church of the Creed finds, or so I believe, institutional embodiment in the assembly gathered around the holder of the office of Peter.

Chalice of God is an attempt to decant the wisdom of the various authors—primarily Catholic, but also Orthodox and Anglican—studied by the present writer in a working lifetime. (Absence of their names in footnotes, in certain cases, should not be taken as implying they have not shaped my thinking.) From the standpoint of its *form*, the aim of my corpus (see the list of titles presented above and their categorization) has always been to explore the riches of Tradition so as to present the faith as an organic whole that is characterised by divine-human truth, beauty, and goodness. My output has used, philosophically, elements of both metaphysical and phenomenological approaches and, theologically, both rational-scholastic and imagistic-poetic modes of discourse. The objective has been to show how divine revelation emerges in human experience and thought as *coherently epiphanic* in character; that is, as manifesting a superabundant fullness of truth, beauty, and goodness, which exceeds those available by other routes. In this way, the incarnate revelation of the Trinity, from which issues the doxological life of the Church, provides the ultimate overall context in which all other reality is to be viewed.

From the standpoint of the *content* of my corpus, the beginning (in 1980) was enquiry into Jesus Christ as the supreme divine artwork which irradiates, so Christian theology and iconography attest, not only the biblical history but human existence and cosmic nature too. From there the work moved out to consider the rational-experiential basis of belief in God and the content of Christian faith, both in its catechetical building blocks and in its ecclesial-dogmatic structure, as well as the theological method best suited to its exploration ("Foundations of the Faith"). That project required for its realisation study of the range and depth of theological tradition, not only as found in pre-modern writers but in those moderns who saw themselves as engaged in recycling, albeit with new insights, that tradition's stored-up wealth ("Theological *Ressourcement*"). It took the liturgy as a key locus for theology and Church, and it treated culture as the field of the world that a Gospel expressed doxologically must transform ("Cult and Culture"). Finally, for the reintegration of a catholicity impaired by Christian disunity, the concern has been to repatriate elements of Eastern Orthodox and Anglican theology, and this in a perspective which, without infidelity to the doctrine of the Roman magisterium, encourages reunion with Constantinople and, in a more limited sense, Christians formed by the patrimony of Anglicanism ("Ecumenical Evaluation").

Aidan Nichols
Blackfriars, Cambridge
Passiontide, 2011

Source: M. V. Alpatov, *Early Russian Icon Painting* (Moscow: Iskusstvo, 1984), plate 165.

Chapter 1

Prolegomena

Dionysius, St. Gregory the Theologian
Russian State Museum, St. Petersburg

I place this enterprise under the patronage of St. Gregory Nazianzen, called by the Eastern Church "the Theologian." The theological approach of my "manifesto" or "systematics in outline" mirrors Gregory's by its integration of philosophy and theology within a consciously ecclesial and indeed liturgical context. For me as for him, in both revelation and theology concepts and images are employed together in the service at once of reasoned understanding and of doxology, the praise of God's glory.

1.1   *A Basic Concept of Theology*

I take systematics to be one possible embodiment of theology at large. I understand theology to be the disciplined exploration of revelation, where the term "disciplined" connotes the application to revelation of the modes of human understanding when exercised at their highest pitch. I hold that the content of revelation is made available by the resources found in Scripture and Tradition, with, as aids to the discernment thereof, the distinctively Christian experience generated by the *sensus fidelium* and, ultimately, the ecclesial magisterium, whose task it is to test that experience by authoritative judgment as well as to forward it by proclamation and teaching as an expression of Tradition. Theology so understood, though affirming the uniqueness of its cognitive standing, also requires the practice of philosophy, from which it draws certain prior affirmations about nature and existence and, not least, about the Source of nature and the Goal of existence in God.

1.1.1 On Scripture and Tradition, I stress their inseparability and the role of the fathers, the historic liturgies, and iconography in establishing the bearings of biblical revelation. I shall speak more of Scripture in chapter 3 and of Tradition in chapter 4.

1.1.2 On the *sensus fidelium*, I emphasise its constitution by the revelation given in Scripture and Tradition. Formally speaking, it differs not at all from the *sensus fidei* of the Church as Bride of Christ. I radically distinguish my position from those who would understand the "sense of the faithful" as the fruit of contemporary human experience, registered as public opinion. The "sense of faith" of each person derives from the spiritual anointing of baptismal grace (cf. 1 John 2:20, 27), and it is exercised within the communion of all the faithful, in a universality of both time and space, since the "faith" in question is that of the whole Church. I draw attention to the importance for its operation of connaturality with divine realities. Along with the monastic theologians of the twelfth century, I consider such connatural knowledge to be grounded in an affinity with the divine disclosure as its recipient's nature is made "like to God" through grace.[1] Such connaturality with divine things "results from the charity which unites us to God: 'he who is joined to the Lord is one spirit with him.' "[2] Within the body of the faithful, especial weight is to be attached, therefore, to the testimonies of the saints. The spirituality of the saints is authority bearing for theological dogmatics.[3] I do not necessarily ascribe value to "spirituality" in general, since I follow St. Athanasius in treating piety (*eusebeia*) as essentially dependent on the orthodox understanding of faith, itself embodied in the Tradition of faith and worship derived from the apostles (cf. 1 Tim 3:15-16).[4] While a theology is "inadequate if it does not end in mysticism, in a living encounter with the living God,"[5] in systematics it suffices to show how the spirituality of the saints enters into the circle of theological thought.

1.1.3   I foreground the role of the ecclesial magisterium in identifying, through doctrinal *proclamation and definition*, the contours of the revelation that generates the *sensus fidelium*. I distinguish myself from those for whom only solemn judgments of ecumenical councils, or of popes speaking *ex cathedra*, have authority in the construction of theological doctrine ("definition"). It should be recalled that, in Catholic Christianity, the guidance of the Spirit is also accorded to the ordinary magisterium of the Church, whether universal or that of the see of Rome in the succession of its pastors, and this attaches not to some isolated act but to a teaching found in the simultaneous or continuous convergence of a plurality of affirmations or explanations ("proclamation"), no one of which, however, could bring positive certitude if taken by itself alone. Though, in the wake of the classical German philosophers, I am committed to a high estimate of rationality (*Vernunft*), I do not consider the charge of "dogmatism" an insult; I hold doctrine to be an intellectual intuition of the mind that anticipates the banquet of the Kingdom in the vision of God, and thus it is "aretegenic," or excellence promoting, since all such anticipation effects human transformation in the direction of salvation, which is the enjoyment of the supreme Good.

1.1.4 I regard the pluralism of Catholic theology as both the de facto historical case and the de jure right of Christian thought, which may take up a variety of starting points in scanning the noetic whole. Though the integration into a single whole of all legitimate theologies is an eschatological desideratum, it can only be approached asymptotically in time. I note that the Church has never required in her schools absolute unity of thought.[6] In any given example, a theology will establish its own profile by the manner in which it selects and arranges in a hierarchy philosophical and theological concepts and themes, seeking to organize its content in their light. It is the work of historical theology to investigate and record this process. I name the selection and hierarchisation involved the establishing of the "philosophical and theological principles of order" (cf. 1.2; 1.3–1.3.2; 1.4–1.4.2).

1.2   The Specificity of Systematics

So far I have laid out my basic concept of theology (while delegating to chapters 3 and 4 a fuller account of Scripture and Tradition). It is the specifying feature of systematics that, compared with other forms of theology, it pays greatly enhanced attention to the philosophical and theological principles of order. This is because systematics wishes to highlight not only the rational coherence of its enterprise but also its character as a nexus of conceptually articulated interrelations that add up to a totality for thought.

1.2.1 A systematics highlights both rationality's wide scope and revelation's comprehensive coherence. The idea of God belongs to reason. Indeed, the idea of God as found within reason posits God as the author of reason (since God is the author of all things, including the laws of thought),to which the Church, in receipt of a sacral thinking more penetrating as well as even more comprehensive in scope, adds that God is also the author of just such sacral understanding, that is, of revelation in its noetic aspect. I consider that the coincidence of the origin of reason, on the one hand, and of the revelation laid out in Catholic theology, on the other, enables us to call the Christian religion "absolute religion," religion in spirit and truth.[7]

1.2.2 My use of the word "sacral" may be questioned; I justify it by saying it refers globally to the way the infinity of the divine manifests itself to finite human beings.

1.3   A Philosophical Principle of Order

A philosophical principle of order in theology serves two offices. The first is common to all versions of such a principle.

It consists in supplying a systematics with its conceptual repertoire. The second is distinctive to this or that version of systematics as found in this or that author. In the case of the present writer, it will consist in identifying the family of concepts deemed most able to render the range of being at large (which corresponds to the scope of reason), and at the same time most able efficaciously to serve the presentation of the realities theology describes (which corresponds to sacral thinking, with its enlarged space).

1.3.1   How, then, would I describe the philosophical principle of order in the particular outline of systematics I am attempting here? In accordance with the defining metaphor of this systematics embodied in its title, *Chalice of God*, I choose to deploy a philosophical principle of order that will exhibit the world as a beautiful receptacle for the gift to creatures of the divine life. The philosophical principle of order corresponding to this description will entail an ontology approached phenomenologically in a primarily aesthetic manner and treating as key the concepts of being, cosmos, history, form, and person.

1.3.2   I concede that, materially speaking, the selection of this approach to philosophy is influenced by my acceptance of revelation (it is an example of a "Christian philosophy"). But I do not regard this as in itself a dereliction of philosophical duty. While disclaiming a philosophical vocation, I consider that my choice exemplifies the following claims by a professional philosopher: "Reason alone underdetermines coherence, and it does not give one's belief system a style. Religious faith helps to produce such a style, and that is probably why the minds of the greatest theistic philosophers of the past are interesting in a way that is rare among the more arid minds of even the best non-theists."[8]

1.4   A Theological Principle of Order

A systematics needs not only a philosophical principle of order but a strictly theological one as well. All theological principles of order will make it their task to present the overall content of theology in the light of some major theme or themes drawn from within that content. It will be the contention of any given theology that the preferred theme yields especially satisfactory results when taken as furnishing the primordial perspective in which revelation is viewed. This the chosen perspective will do if it enables all aspects of revelation, the source of sacral thought, to be illuminatingly displayed and, moreover, interrelated in organic fashion. German romantic theology, to which, in this regard, I declare a debt, has termed this the "encyclo-paedic" imperative, emphasizing the origin of that adjective in the noun "circle," and explaining the subjacent notion by appeal to the idea of organism. "Organism is a completed circle of living relationships which mutually determine and verify each other."[9] In theological science, so conceived, what is particular is possessed only in the whole—that is, in the system. In the circle of doctrines can be found no truth which, as such, is unnecessary, and yet each truth is free for itself, since the necessity in question arises "from the whole and from the inner relationships in which each truth stands towards the others, completing them and determining them" as it does so.[10]

1.4.1 What theological principle of order have I chosen? In keeping with the metaphor found in this book's title (cf. 1.3.1), I select a theological principle of order which finds the heart of Christian revelation in the outpouring of plenitude on the world (cf. 2.4.3), through the self-emptying of the Holy Trinity in Jesus Christ whereby a reconciling and deifying share in divine life is accorded us.

1.4.2 The writing of systematics is feasible, but not because philosophy can supply the adequate ontological undertow for fully comprehensive thought. Here, I register a refusal to allow philosophy rights of governance over theology. Systematics is, rather, a feasible intellectual exercise because it is the case that in history God himself has revealed his all-round relations with the world. God has thus enabled the raids of reason on the intelligible to be unified by the influence of his Spirit around the centre that is his incarnate Word. Here, I affirm the capacity of orthodox theology to restructure the insights of rationality in what is, pre-eschatologically, the fullest conceivable way. In so saying, I also affirm the primacy of the theological principle of order in systematics—though I insist as well on the indispensability of its accompanying philosophical counterpart. I do not consider that the concept of systematics transgresses the mysteric character of revelation; I shall describe in chapter 4 how I understand "mystery" (cf. 4.1–4.1.3), but meanwhile I note how I have already accepted as authority bearing for theology at large the spiritual experience of the saints (cf. 1.1.2).

Source: R. Grierson, ed., *Gates of Mystery: The Art of Holy Russia*
(Fort Worth, TX: Intercultura, 1994), p. 115.

Chapter 2

A Congruent Ontology

Novgorod School, The Old Testament Trinity
Russian State Museum, St. Petersburg

In the Theophany at the Oak of Mamre (Gen 18:1-16), Abraham and Sarah's angelic visitors make manifest the creative Trinity. They appear in this icon gesturing toward golden vessels, the central one of which contains the head of a sacrificed calf. In such icons of the Trinity it is usual to interpret the angel on the left as the Father, the angel on the right as the Spirit, the angel in the centre as the Son. In the perspective of our study, the icon represents the divine establishment of the world as a receptacle for God's blessing and, in particular, the filling of the chalice of the world with the redemptive grace of the Sacrifice of Christ.

2.1   *Preamble*

Following my principles of order, a suitable ontology for systematics must be congruent in both of two senses at the same time: it must meet the needs of philosophy, as indicated by the notion of being as "beautiful receptacle," and those of theology, as given in the idea of the "plenary outpouring" of divine life. Only through meeting both demands simultaneously, if in different respects, can an ontology suited to systematics be crafted.

2.2   *An Ontology Suited to the Demands of Philosophy*

The notion of being as "beautiful receptacle" is applicable in two directions. First, it must apply to the being of nature. Second, it must apply to what is most metaphysically differentiated in nature, the being of persons—as unfolded in time, we call that their "existence," the *telos* of which, so revelation of the call to divinization allows us to affirm, is not exhausted by the natural good. The being of nature is a fine structure for receiving fresh influxes of being (this is the message of scientific cosmology); the being of persons is a fine structure for receiving not only fresh influxes of creaturely being but inflow from the Source of being itself (this is the message—as I interpret it—of personalist Existentialism, for which the scope of human possibility is more than the actualization of our present potentialities). This difference between the cosmological and the personal applications of my foundational notion of being as "beautiful receptacle" is highly significant: it points to the unique place occupied by hypostases within the world order as a whole.

2.2.1 The concept of receptacle allows us to situate ontology in a theistic context. The being of the world is so constituted as to receive. This statement falls into two portions. First, the being of the world is *constituted*: the world is a primordial setting in being and hence a dependent reality; second, this constituted being of the world is a *receiving* kind of being: it continues to be marked in its development by the nature of its origin, and its being can be called, therefore, abiding participation in an original gift.

2.2.2 I claim my philosophy as a version of Thomism, distinctive through two emphases: by its emphasis on the phenomenologically aesthetic character of the natural world, as well as in its stress on the capacity of emergent form, when hypostatic in quality, to receive the divine. It is, then, a realism for which I have already described the following notions as key: being (encountered most strikingly in aesthetic appearance), cosmos, history, form, and personhood (cf. 1.3.1). In the present historical conjuncture, I accept that for minds to recover their ordinate relation to being, the classical Christian-Hellenic inheritance of the "perennial philosophy" may need to be married with a "prudent romanticism" in which the intuitive roots of human contact with the extramentally real can be refreshed by the disciplined use of the imagination. The romanticism I have in mind is well exemplified in the work of Samuel Taylor Coleridge, who asked his readers: "Hast thou ever raised thy mind to the consideration of EXISTENCE, in and by itself, as the mere act of existing? Hast thou ever said to thyself, thoughtfully, IT IS! heedless in that moment, whether it were a man before thee, or a flower, or a grain of sand? . . . If thou hast indeed attained to this, thou wilt have felt the presence of a mystery."[1]

2.2.3 I would justify my marriage of Aquinas with the romantics in the following way. The question at stake is how to perceive things as pointing by "contuition" to their divine Source. I proceed in four steps, the first three of which will also lay out my fundamental ontology. *First*, with St. Thomas, I affirm that metaphysics should begin with an apprehension of things as *habens esse*, "having being," and thus a grasp by judgment of the *esse* of things. Anything in its nature—itself expressible by the human mind in a concept, since each existent possesses form—is essentially a "be-ing."[2] But things have being precisely by receiving it. Anything whose nature does not demand its existence (*esse*) must have its being from another—meaning, ultimately, from the First Cause.[3] As modes of being— for all things are composites of a nature with an "act of being," *actus essendi*—things add to being not by bringing to it something extrinsic but, on the contrary, by bringing out of it its intrinsic riches in some determinate way. In the Thomist school, no contrast sets at odds the being of things and their appearance; rather, as surfaced from the depths of being, things open into the light. *Second*, I note that the consequence of receiving in some determinate manner the *actus essendi* is a flow of self-communication— to whatever extent possible for this nature or that. Self-expression through activity (not only inward but also, and especially, outward) is the natural perfection, the flowering, of being.[4] According to the Thomist adage, substance is *for the sake of* operation; being as existing in itself naturally turns toward others in its self-communicating activity (and this is preeminently true of beings that are personal, of hypostases).[5] *Third*, I acknowledge here a tacit reference to the divine, since effects must carry a trace of affinity with their causes. To know beings is implicitly to know God, since all things are in some manner likenesses of divine being, which, in its communicative outflow in creation, shows itself for what it is. Through a doctrine of participation (to be a likeness is to share, in some manner, the features of one's Cause), such recognition paves the way to a view of all existents, individually and in their cosmic unity, in their dependence on God. Things, then, mirror their Source, enjoying a status which Plato (especially) deployed a varied vocabulary to express.[6] Yet in a twenty-first-century Western context, not only is reason overvalued vis-à-vis faith, whose own potential for suggesting metaphysical insight is unthinkingly rejected. Worse, reason itself is narrowly conceived, since it is defined exclusively either in terms of logical procedures or in those of its instrumental role in science and technology. Reason is treated as alien to desire, feeling, religion, art (cf. introduction). In this setting, therefore—and here I take my *fourth* step—poetic intelligence may be necessary for apprehending things in their substantial, participatory, dependent being. And that is so not least when the world's being is most basically described as "beautiful receptacle."

2.2.4 In any case, the act-of-being of what exists—as distinct from its essence—always lies beyond conceptual thinking and can best be gestured toward poetically. The interplay of concept and image is, therefore, vital to my project, which, accordingly, is neither rationalist nor purely poetic.

2.2.5 Indeed, well beyond the bifurcation of concept and image, I subscribe to the illuminationism of Thomas for which the mind produces truth, owing, first and fore-most, not to its conceptual capacity or to its imaginative power but to its possession of "natural light."[7] On contact with sensuous experience, the intellect is able to generate first principles, and, with their help, it gradually builds up what it knows. But it is thus able to construct truth only because it is itself a participation in Truth. The mind *is* the light of divine truth—analogically speaking, by way of participation. It is a participated likeness of the uncreated light in which the ideas of all things dwell. This is, I hold, the only genuine antidote to scepticism and the sole au-thentic foundationalism. Participated divine light, existing as finite mind, intimately united with the body, precedes all the data of perception and makes apprehension of their inner order and meaning possible.

2.2.6 I note how this has practical presuppositions and corollaries germane to my purpose. I am Platonist enough to think knowledge is not simply propositional, expressive of intellectual judgment, but involves a turning of the soul toward what is truly good, and thus it combines cognitive and volitional elements in a single act. The natural constitution of mind already suggests its ultimate orderedness through faith to grace and glory. "'The reve-lation of faith is a discovery [i.e., uncovering] of itself by the Divine reason, the unveiling of the Divine Intelli-gence, and the illumination flowing from it cast upon the intelligence of man.'"[8] Human knowing can be supernatu-rally elevated so as to share more deeply in the Wisdom of God. Systematics requires this fundamental elevation of the structure of knowing; revelation generates a theo-logical conception of knowing as existential encounter with God and personal participation, through the Holy

Spirit, in the transfigured humanity of Christ as he stands before the Father. Systematics also calls for that contemplative exercise which is the unfolding of the life of faith in all its credal, sacramental, and mystical dimensions (cf. 1.1–1.1.2).

2.2.7 Since I have made "person" a key concept in my philosophical repertoire, I must note that a philosophy appropriate to the needs of the hypostatic order in ontology will culminate in an account of the openness of persons to absolute, and not merely relative, transcendence. Though personal substance is ordered to relationship in a stronger sense than any other natural kind of substance, the range of personal acts is not limited by the social realm or indeed the ecosphere. It is, rather, indefinitely open. By understanding that openness as sharing in the possibility of a further gift, lying beyond the cosmic order, even in its hypostatic culmination, a philosophical ontology will look ahead to the requirements of a properly theological ontology, when the "chalice of God" is filled.

2.3   The Key Ontological Terms

I must now clothe these claims with more flesh. Each of the key terms used (cf. 1.3.1; 2.2.2) requires some elucidation.

2.3.1 Though I have already indicated my doctrine of being (cf. 2.2.1; 2.2.3), I wish to affirm my agreement with the movement called "Radical Orthodoxy" in its privileging of the categories of participation and mediation. I hold that being is a commonwealth, fundamentally hospitable to sharing and, therefore, bestowing. Though the ultimate rationale for this is Trinitarian, it can also be stated for its own sake. Participation is a causal relation which explains, at various levels, the coexistence of the one and the many, and where metaphysical range is at its most comprehensive, it denotes a relation of God to everything else.[9] Behind the "many" that share in something common, there has to be a "one," and where perfection is concerned (that which it is better to have than not to have and which does not entail any kind of limit), the single source *is* the perfection, whilst the many are composed of the perfection received and something else.[10] The capacity of the participating to mediate a share in perfection to others is the hallmark of the commonwealth of being. (That is so even though the highest application of the concept of participation is found in the order of grace, which is where the power of God to enable participations of himself initiates creatures into his own intimate life.) I consider the interrelated notions of participation and mediation to offer an ontology of incomparable suppleness, allowing for great subtlety in the description of causal structures. Mediation can itself be submediated, and participations allow of further participations internal to themselves. It is a prime principle of Thomism to affirm that creaturely substances enjoy the dignity of true causes. I note how this is an axiom which also warrants a principle of hierarchy or internal ordering, in dignity and value, of the beings in the world. Such a hierarchy may, however, be complex in its functioning. (Thus, for example, within the order of grace, in the suborder of charismatic holiness, St. Birgitta of Sweden may be placed above her interlocutor Pope Gregory XI, who in turn, in the suborder of sacramentally founded office, stands above her.) At the same time, the ontology I favour respects the divine transcendence through its use of the idioms of negation and excess to indicate the difference between the being of the many and the being of the One—who is "not" the many (negation) and who is "more than" (excess) everything else. I salute the aspiration of the unknown Syrian monk who wrote as "Dionysius the Areopagite" in seeking to integrate this neoplatonic insight into sacred doctrine, thereby indicating the radical differentiation and utter inequality that holds between God and the world. Thus, since the divine One is the "Cause of all beings, we should posit and ascribe to it all the affirmations we make in regard to beings, [yet nevertheless] more appropriately, we should negate all these affirmations, since it surpasses all beings."[11] I ought to add that such differentiation and inequality is further deepened by the mystery of sin which not only distinguishes but alienates creatures from the divine (cf. 2.3.6; 5.6.2–5.6.3).

2.3.2 I turn now to the "phenomenologically aesthetic character" of the world. Phenomenology is the disciplined attempt to describe and analyse the immediate data of awareness as they are given to consciousness. A rich description of things as they enter into human experience will privilege the aesthetic response, since the latter is concerned with both surprise at how things appear to us to be and admiration at their formal organization. When as human beings we reflect on our natural attitudes—which might be embodied in, say, Ruskin's writing on the geological scene or Hopkins's evocations of cloud formation—we disengage thought about how we are participants in the world and its manifestations. The phenomenologically aesthetic response to the world is, "This is how it appears, and as such it is wonderful!" This is my version of the claim of Plato that coming into contact with the beautiful is the way we begin to recognize the call of "the Good," which is not just the moral good but that which can satisfy all our intellectual, spiritual, and even physical needs in a unified experience. In the complexity, yet concreteness and experiential unity of such wonder, no other immediate knowledge, given in direct acts, is so striking or wide-ranging in its implications. I take this to be the primal instance of discovered objectivity. In Plato's terminology, thanks to the partial beauties open to the senses, the form of Beauty is more accessible than are the other forms.[12] When the Source and Goal of being is accessed by adhesion to Trinitarianism (cf. 6.4.3), the full implications of aesthetic wonder will become plain.

2.3.3   What, then, of "cosmos"? The presupposition of all fruitful scientific thought, echoed in the Thomist metaphysic (cf. 2.2.3), is that how things appear to us to be is how they are—and thus how they will behave, as they enter into what are, often enough, measurable relations within an interlocking order of the kind we call a cosmos. The same epistemological realism which encourages the natural scientist to go beyond a phenomenological approach to experience, so as to make an affirmation of cosmic order, leads his philosophical colleague to consider the non-self-sufficiency of the cosmos, and hence its contingency, which concept entails, as the obverse of the coin, the necessity of that on which the cosmos depends. The existence of contingent being must be explained by something that in itself is noncontingent. In the words of a British astronomer royal, "Theorists may, some day, be able to write down fundamental equations governing physical reality. But physics can never explain what 'breathes fire' into the equations, and actualizes them in a real cosmos,"[13] for this is—we should add—the *actus essendi*, the endlessly participable divine act of communicating being. That in turn justifies the notion of the being of the world as essentially received being, a key element in my "chalice" concept (cf. 2.2.1). A sacral cosmology (one that affirms the mediation of the infinite by the finite [cf. 1.2.2]) is thus made possible, and it will note how in various religions the same natural symbols (as, for example, sun, sky, rain) symbolize similar realities; the affinities they indicate are rooted in the analogy of being and the permanent structures of the human spirit. The objectivity of religion at large lies in the connexion of things not only among themselves but with the divine, which itself is aboriginally posited together with the very idea of the world (cf. 1.2.1).[14] A world so constituted may be expected to carry a variety of signals of transcendence; diverse arguments for the existence of God put forward in the tradition of Christian thought draw much of their suasive force from the experiential traces such signals leave. My concept of cosmos is sufficiently broad-minded to include the possibility of extraterrestrial intelligence; I would link to this the realm of the angelic (cf. 2.4.4). The intuition that there is intelligent life elsewhere in the universe, while running ahead of physical evidence, I count as a surmise of the copresence of the angels.

2.3.4　My next key term is "history." The world order is launched on a temporal process, of which the two chief facets are physical evolution and the emergence of persons who act in relation to their inherited environment as free makers of change—or what we term "history." *Evolution* does not contradict the reception of being from its Source since chance events can be subsumed under divine providence. Chance itself is subject to statistical lawfulness, the long-term outcomes of which are predictable with some certainty (not, however, that God predicts; rather, he *under-stands*). That some causal factors are statistical in character does not eliminate, then, the aitiological certainties of divine providence in a world where statistical laws and deterministic laws intermesh. The cosmic story combines both novelty and regularity. Organized patterns emerge which produce new qualitative syntheses that could not have been predicted from knowledge of the constituent elements of the pattern before they were so organized. *History* continues the process of such a world by other means. Those other means are the agency of human beings in their limited yet real freedom of manoeuvre. I understand historiography to be ultimately a theological enterprise, and those for whom history has already all but achieved its end (Marxists and Liberals) or, conversely, lacks any rhyme or reason (postmodernists) are disqualified from adequate generalization about its course. I take history to be primally salvation history, that is, the constantly reconfigured positioning of humanity vis-à-vis the self-disclosing God of grace who is at work in both corporate culture and individual human decision until the story reaches its consummating End (cf. 5.9). The sign of such reconfigured positioning is enhancement of both understanding and practice, analogous with the qualitative advance entailed in the arrival of new emergents in the cosmos. This I term "transformation" (cf. 2.3.5). It is both an elevation of our species and its repair, for the historical process testifies to the metaphysical incongruity of man's place in the cosmos. Man's self-destructiveness and failure to attain a *telos* that cures dissatisfaction suggest a disjunction in his origins to which, theologically, the name "original sin" is applied (cf. 2.4.5; 5.6.2–5.6.3).

2.3.5 "Form" refers to the structured intelligibility of things, which manifests itself in their self-presentation to the perceiver. The beauty and goodness of reality is based on its form, though in different fashions, since beauty is concerned with the knowledge of what delights, goodness with what satisfies our appetite for some end. The concept of form is, I venture, flexible enough to allow of multiple transpositions: it may refer to a substance or to the relations integral to that substance (both of these have to do with primordial form), or to its concrete condition (its actual form), or to the nature of its ideal fulfillment (which, when divinely underpinned, is definitive, "eschatological," form). "Transformation" (cf. 2.3.4), change of form by enhancement of some original beauty or goodness, is a required term for how, within the historical process, existents may themselves be transposed to a new and better manner of being. This is especially pertinent to the condition of persons (cf. 2.3.6).

2.3.6 My final key term must indeed be "personhood." The idea of "being a person" arises, I take it, from human beings' reflection on the experience of how they are themselves qua originators of love and understanding in relation to others like them. Personhood bespeaks a unique spiritual value for each of us. Though the concept appeared comparatively late in the history of thought, any attempt to go back behind it would widely be recognized as temerarious, so crucial is it for the defence of human dignity, integrity, responsibility, rights. While the term allows—more, entails—accepting the social nature of the individual (his or her intersubjectivity) and the necessity of social recognition, it forbids regarding the person as reducible to sociality or dependent on social acknowledgement.

A self may be what I experience; a person is what I am. Personhood is unique for each one, with a depth of mystery that mirrors in its own way the divine incomprehensibility. True, the common nature of man, as well as its universal characteristics, are caught up in all movement toward the human *telos*. Yet the uniqueness of persons is not adequately expressed by the instantiation of common nature alone. Though as mind-body composites we are embedded in the natural order, we are not, for all that, confined to its range. The hypostatic order declares itself in its difference from the order of nature at large. Its metaphysical sign is the immateriality and hence immortality of the human soul, whose highest powers are love and understanding. The interruption in the natural realm produced by the emergence of the hypostatic order is negatively signaled by the appearance of true unintelligibility: the surd that is human sin and which requires personal responsibility—or, rather, irresponsibility—for its committal. Unlike chance events, sin falls outside the divine understanding since it is objectively unintelligible, a falling away from being. Positively, however, personhood marks what is highest in created being,[15] since the powers of love and understanding make possible a relationality—communicativity together with receptivity—only dimly adumbrated in other creatures. Such relationality indicates how persons belong together in the macrosociety of the polis and the microsociety of the household and the circle of friends (cf. 5.7.1–5.7.2). And it points ultimately to the human vocation to be images of the Holy Trinity (cf. 6.4.3); I uphold a "theomorphic anthropology."

2.3.7   In all this, I presume a "fiducial" attitude to language.[16] Language does not lead us astray in its rendering of those aspects of the world which prompt it. Deconstructionists who claim otherwise evidently have themselves a secret (and contradictory) trust in language, or by what criterion could they say (I stress the word "say") that language commonly leads us astray from truth? This fiducial embrace includes, importantly, metaphor; the conspiracy of metaphorical and more coolly literal language can render, not exhaustively yet aright so far as it goes, the realities it seeks to describe. Only on this presupposition can I agree with analytic philosophers, dominant in our Anglophone culture, that the goal of philosophy is the analysis of the structure of thought by means of analyzing language. Just as sacral cosmologies read the cosmic order as a fabric woven of natural symbols, so, congruently and in a manner I welcome, romanticism developed its notion of the symbol-in-language as that form of language in which something becomes accessible that is otherwise beyond our reach.[17]

2.4   An Ontology Suited to the Demands of Theology

I note the judicious comment of Bl. John Paul II, that while "the human search for truth—philosophy, pursued in keeping with its own rules—can only help to understand God's word better . . . [t]heology's source and starting-point must always be the word of God revealed in history, while its final goal will be an understanding of that word which increases with each passing generation."[18]

2.4.1 I have said (cf. 2.1) that a suitable ontology must also meet the needs of theology and not those of philosophy alone. A theological ontology is concerned with "plenary outpouring," filling up the chalice of the world in human persons and their environments. The unified vision of reality that human wisdom seeks can now—since the Incarnation—only be attained on the basis of a faith that takes its bearings from the self-revelation of God in the Logos made human. Here, as John Paul II puts it, "the Eternal has entered time," and thus, in words which seem to echo a key phrase used by Hans Urs von Balthasar, "the whole lies hidden in the part."[19] The phrase "the Logos made human" comprises two elements: affirmation of the divine Logos, the pattern maker of the world, and hence the doctrine of creation; and assertion of his Incarnation or enmanment, and hence a doctrine of new creation in the embodied Word. As to *creation*: God makes created participations of his being exist outside himself, and he does so "in time" in the sense that "the eternal God has eternally willed that something 'other' than himself should originate with a beginning of its temporal existence."[20] Following St. Maximus Confessor, I can agree that, thanks to the divine creative act, "in its origins and destiny, reality is theandric: having participation in the Logos as its principle and goal, it is destined to be brought into unity through the priestly mediatorial agency of humanity."[21] And as to *new creation*, for the same Byzantine Church father, "this process is fulfilled through the Incarnation, death, and resurrection of the Word who has brought into mutual harmony and all-embracing unity the various levels of creaturely reality."[22]

2.4.2 Philosophy must, therefore, be oriented to theology, since outside the mystery of Christ—which is the mystery of the Trinity in its saving outreach to mankind—the "mystery of personal existence remains an insoluble riddle."[23] The divine truth proposed to us in the Scriptures and interpreted by the Church's Tradition-based teaching enjoys an "innate intelligibility" that provides the consistency that is proper to a body of wisdom[24] and so renders theology capable of comparison with philosophical wisdom to which, owing both to its directly divine source and to its own comprehensive character, it enjoys a relation of superordination (cf. 1.4.2). That supremacy is exercised, however, as a "constitutional" rule whereby philosophy retains, in its union with theology, a due autonomy. I accept a "Chalcedonian" model for the interconnexion of philosophy and theology, whereby they are related without confusion but also without separation.[25]

2.4.3 I maintain that the cumulative force of the biblical texts that bear on ontological value is well described in terms of the "plenary outpouring" crucial to my "chalice" concept. Such texts concern the divine freedom which manifests the plenitude of being as it seeks to bestow itself on man; the "riches of [the Father's] glorious inheritance in the saints" (Eph 1:18), accorded through Christ Jesus in whom "all the fulness of God was pleased to dwell, and through him to reconcile to himself all things, whether on earth or in heaven, making peace by the blood of his cross" (Col 1:19-20), which libation is the flow of grace, the "river of the water of life, bright as crystal, flowing from the throne of God and of the Lamb" (Rev 22:1), such that even now "from his fulness have we all received, grace upon grace" (John 1:16). Since the human person is the climactic site for encounter with being in its fountainhead (he or she is the animal that practices metaphysical contemplation), the decisive divine intervention in the world order, in its historical process, appropriately—if also

amazingly—took the form of Incarnation, the assumption
of manhood into God. The Greek fathers, therefore, rightly
call Incarnation *enanthrôpêsis*: God's "becoming man."
Metaphysics is renewed by Christology in the form of
meta-anthropology—always remembering, however, that,
as the crown of the cosmos, humankind in its own created
fullness can never be separated from the living environment to which man enjoys so many ties in other created
beings, whether animal, vegetable, or mineral.

2.4.4 I note that for Scripture the cosmos in its intelligent aspect is not confined to *homo sapiens*. As the
rational species on this planet emerges, it enters an environment already penetrated by intellectuality (cf. 2.3.3).
It appears in a cosmos where intelligence is disposed either
to offer the adoring praise of unconditional theocentricity
(in the holy angels) or to exult in the prideful abuse of
understanding through which other angels "fell." As if in
compensation for such spiritual conflict, innocence covers
the animals. For Scripture, a cosmic covenant extends to
beasts. Psalms 104 and 148 bespeak the worthiness before
their Creator of the animals of the field, the creatures of
the sea, and the birds of the air.[26]

2.4.5 A theological ontology will take its cue not only
from creation but also from new creation in the Paschal
Mystery, for the latter, by the way it brings the Incarnation
of God in creation to its climax, constitutes revelation's
true centre. The mystery of the life-giving kenosis of God-
in-Christ is structured analogically with the metaphysical
mystery of being which, as exhibited in creation, is so full
that it can make itself poor, giving itself away by pouring
itself out into existents. The divine gift of being has its

culmination in the Cradle of Bethlehem and, in definitive fashion, on the Cross of Calvary. There, the total generosity of God is made manifest in an extreme of humility, God himself overcoming all man's alienation—through enduring it in the humanized hypostasis of the Son—so as to bring humankind to the fullness of life. "I came that they may have life, and have it abundantly" (John 10:10). Thus the disjunction at human origins (cf. 2.3.4), in and from the anonymous protoparent "Adam," is made good, whilst at the same time man's mode of being is not only repaired but innovatively transformed.

2.4.6   This must mean a Trinitarian ontology, which I understand as an expansion of the patristic doctrine of the *vestigia Trinitatis* and not—as some would critically comment—an attempt to advertise the "relevance" of Trinitarianism to innerworldly concerns, for (so I claim) I have no such concerns that are not already thought through in relation to revelation. Only via the doctrine of the Trinity, which reveals that God is abundantly relational in himself, can it been seen in what way, congruently with his own intimate life, he creates a world that is distinct from him yet sheltered in his love. Indeed, his eternally realized love as Father, Son, and Holy Spirit means that ontological thinking should always begin from the gift of a plenitude—in sharpest contrast to Hegel's thought for which the fullness of the Absolute is a goal to be gained through the process of history. The act whereby God lavishes being does not itself subsist but terminates in creatures in which—so it now appears from the Trinitarian revelation in Christ—the goodness of God inheres as generosity in love (cf. 2.2.1; 2.2.3; 2.3.1; 6.2.5; 6.4.3). The Giver has communicated himself in the gift of being in such a way that the creative act reaches to the core of the creature's freedom. Thus, not only is the gift character of creation grounded in the Trinity; that gift character also points to the mystery of grace whereby human freedom is enfolded in a divine transforming act which justifies, sanctifies, deifies, and thereby ushers creatures into the life of God. The act whereby God consummates the gift of being in the new creation that flows from the Word Incarnate's Paschal Mystery is love in a higher and more intimate sense than with any generosity bestowed in creating. It is the introduction of human freedom into the everlasting love-exchange of the Trinity itself.

2.4.7 Thus Christian revelation confirms and takes further what was already implied by *esse personale* in a world constituted by the receiving of being (2.3.6; 2.2.1). Relationality, which is at once receptivity and communicativity, is built into not only personal acting but personal being itself, for humans are, par excellence, in the image of the Trinitarian Son through whom all things were made—and from whom whatever is remade takes that remaking. As the Son receives all he has from the Father and is thus able to communicate that "all" through their common Spirit, so persons made in his image receive their being prior to acting it out energetically in relation not only to God but to others like themselves. The fruits of the transformation of persons in the New Adam are to be expected in three modes: contingently in a well-ordered Christian polis; essentially but provisionally in the Church; essentially and definitively in the Kingdom of which the well-ordered Christian polis is the shadow and the Church, the inaugural form. I shall in due course make plain that I understand none of these in an extracontemplative fashion or in a way that prescinds from the need for ascesis (cf. 5.4–5.4.1) in holiness of life (cf. 5.6.4), for without an existence stamped by the Christ form, they are impossible (cf. 5.2.1).

2.4.8   Thinking about revelation will, then, typically press into service, but in its own fashion, categories from philosophical (including social-philosophical) thought. It will do so in a way that is not merely dialectical but mystagogical in character. In considering which terms to take over from classical *paideia*, the Church fathers asked whether what is proposed coincides with the experience of faith, prayer, and religious existence generally of the Christian mystery, itself embracing, in its singleness, the different mysteries which this "outline" will later address (see chapter 5). The process whereby terms and formulae are tested is itself an exercise of *eusebeia* (cf. 1.1.2), the piety of the orthodox faith, and it requires prayerful preparation for a successful outcome, as St. Gregory Nazianzen insists in his *First Theological Oration*.[27]

Source: M. V. Alpatov, *Early Russian Icon Painting* (Moscow: Iskusstvo, 1984), plate 64.

Chapter 3

A Christological Determination of Biblical History

Theophanes the Greek (ascribed), The Transfiguration
Tretyakov Gallery, Moscow

The mystery of the Transfiguration (Matthew 17:1-8 and parallels) places the entire ministry of Christ under the sign of the Law and the Prophets, represented by Moses and Elijah. Christ cannot be understood without the Old Testament, nor can the overall thrust of the Old Testament be grasped without Christ. The icon presumes our understanding (in *Chalice of God*) of the saving events narrated in Scripture: genuinely historical, yet at the same time embodying divine action in a cosmos all of whose constituents are dependent on divine being for the ground of their interaction. The Gospel episode it portrays does not close without Jesus pointing ahead to the climax of his mission in his Sacrifice. Meanwhile, the Transfiguration mystery discloses the divinity of the Trinitarian Son.

3.1   A Fundamental Hermeneutic

Along with the fathers of the Church, Catholic exegesis understands the revelation that enables sacral thinking and thus, in union with philosophy, systematics itself (cf. 1.2.1) as given in, with, and through a history whose bearings must be taken from the incarnate Word, Jesus Christ. It is through Christ that the Old Testament becomes theologically pertinent to Gentiles. The faith which joins human beings to Christ also joins them through Christ to the ancient faith of Israel who awaited his coming.

3.1.1 I have rejected the postmodern repudiation of metanarrative (cf. introduction), and indeed in the canonical Bible, the Bible of the Church, a single overarching grand narrative pertains. The biblical text deals with a single revelation, which is at once irreducibly particular and intentionally universal. It concerns the fate of one people, Israel (hence particularity), whose call it is to be the light for all peoples on earth (hence universality). After the emergence of *homo sapiens*, the primary vehicle of divine disclosure in the history that advances the world process turns out to be a particular human "family," but that family is so prepared as to become the means of a new alignment of humanity with God—the outpouring of his Spirit on all flesh—and thus the filling of the world's receptacle with divine life. "This is our God; no other can be compared to him! He found the whole way to knowledge, and gave her to Jacob his servant and to Israel whom he loved. Afterward she appeared upon earth and lived among men" (Bar 3:35-37). Were we to draw from the order of nature a term suited in this regard to the order of grace, we might call Israel "evolutionarily favoured"— though in a reversal of Darwinian expectations the blessing acquired by the salvationally fittest is to be spread to the entire biological stock, humanity in its total extent. That blessing has repercussions that are retroactive as well as contemporaneous and proactive (the Incarnation and Atonement affect past, present, and future).

3.1.2 I disallow radical historical scepticism about the principal events marking the biblical narrative, since a revelation about the meaning of divine acts in history is incoherent without the happening of the events which are the outcome of the acts concerned. In particular, without rejecting some role for oral tradition in the shaping of the literary material, I reiterate the ancient conviction of the Church that the apostles Matthew and John, as eyewitnesses of the Word, and Mark and Luke, as secretaries to Peter and Paul, composed the four canonical Gospels. The recovery of emphasis on personal transmission of eyewitness material, as found in outstanding exegetes of recent years,[1] is a matter for rejoicing. I believe the exaggerated weight placed on the apocryphal Gospels by some modern scholars in their reconstructions of Christian origins to derive from an idealizing of Gnosticism (radically individualist, lacking ecclesial structures, giving apparent prominence to women) in modern Western, and especially North American, academia.[2] Judging that, in accounts of the provenance of the Gospels, especial weight should be given to the earliest subapostolic witnesses, I accept the formula of Clement of Alexandria, resting on the memory of the "very earliest presbyters,"[3] to the effect that the order of the making of the Gospels runs: Matthew, Luke, Mark, John.[4]

3.1.3 It should be stressed that the original Bible of the Church in both East and West was the Greek Septuagint and the Greek New Testament, which is not to deny the utility of the readings found in the Hebrew tradition, first Latinised by St. Jerome in the Vulgate. For this reason, the books called "deuterocanonical" are, as both the Catholic and Orthodox Churches confess, fully authoritative for the biblical testimony to revelation.

3.1.4 With the aid of the Gospels, I take Jesus to be in himself the primary sign of credibility for his own revelation, though secondary signs, not separable from his person and work, are his miracles and fulfillment of prophecy, to which I am willing to add the "sociological miracle" of the Church's genesis, development, and survival. The Christian theologian does not proclaim Israel but Jesus, though he or she recognizes the revelation of God in Israel to be a necessary implication of Jesus' claims.

3.1.5 Whilst I acknowledge the value of philological and, more widely, historical studies for understanding the original setting of biblical texts, when those texts are considered precisely as Scripture, they are, I hold, addressed not primarily to their original hearers but to the ecclesial community—first, for the Jewish Scriptures, Israel, and then, for the entire canon, the apostolic Church, which is their divinely intended recipient. The hermeneutical key to the Scriptures is, as Origen of Alexandria put it, "that rule and discipline delivered by Jesus Christ to the apostles and handed down by them in succession to their posterity."[5] Though the Church cannot judge the Word of God embodied in Scripture, she can and does judge the interpretations human beings offer of God's Word. Scripture is the objective standard in relation to which the Church teaches doctrine, but this means that Scripture needs the

Church for its magisterial proclamation, which itself relies on Tradition, the provider of the "rule of faith," as its interpretative key (cf. 4.2).

3.1.6 The Bible is the Book of the Church not only in the sense that it has the new Israel as its intended corporate reader. It is also the Book of the Church in the sense that its message concerns both Christ and the Church, a King who has a Kingdom. Those who, on the basis of the biblical revelation, affirm that in the life, death, and Resurrection of Christ Israel's destiny is attained and a new covenant between God and humanity, surpassing the creation covenant, is now put in place, proclaim like royal heralds to the world its sovereign Lord. It is by means of a divinely enabled society, the Church, itself the inaugural form of the Kingdom (cf. 2.4.7), that the history of the world can move toward its goal: the communion of persons in the divine life. Their existence is a transformed be-ing which, lost in admiration in the vision of the Trinity (cf. 6.4.3), intensifies to maximal extent aesthetic wonder at the existence of the world (cf. 2.2.2) and dependent participation as the world is in the surpassing fullness of being that is God (cf. 2.2.3).

3.1.7 With the American theologian R. R. Reno,[6] I discount any charge of hermeneutical naïveté since I take the historical distance between the biblical texts and subsequent generations to be not so much a separation as the opening up of a temporal space for the fulfillment of the Scriptures in the Holy Spirit. Thanks to the Spirit of the incarnate Word, the public memory of the community, as expressed in the Creeds, embodied in the doctrine of magisterial teachers, and confirmed by signs of holiness, guides subsequent generations to a grasp of biblical revelation on which the ongoing history of the communion between the Church and her Lord can throw new lights (cf. 4.1–4.1.1).

3.1.8   Likewise, with Reno again, I consider that the metaphysical distance whereby in their limited character the biblical texts, when regarded as divine self-disclosure, can only signal the infinite meaning they carry may itself be Christologically overcome. As disciples of Christ, the faithful are enabled through the eternal Word who became flesh to find that which transcends time and finitude. In Augustine's words, "We would not be able to do this except that Wisdom himself saw fit to make himself congruous with such infirmity as ours."[7] The practice of the hermeneutical approach I sponsor entails submission to spiritual discipline in the common life of the Church, with its worship, asceticism, and mutual service. I emphasise again in this connexion the hermeneutical value of the spirituality of the saints (cf. 1.1.2).

3.2   The Christological Determinant

My Christology is based on what the Church fathers made of the Bible (cf. introduction; 3.1); the moment of the fathers is the moment of the constitutive reception of biblical revelation, which the later Church only excogitates and applies.[8]

3.2.1   Since the revelation to which the biblical texts, as read by the fathers, bear witness is itself a unity, those texts can only be properly read within the (Christocentrically interpreted) canon of Scripture as a whole. Just as on the Mount of the Transfiguration the three selected apostles, in seeing the glorified Christ between Moses and Elijah, understood the Law and the Prophets to be in conversation with him, so at the end of that theophany they "saw no one but Jesus only" (Matt 17:8), since the Law and the Prophets become clear in him as the climax of revelation history (cf. 3.1). Though God transcends all signs, he has rendered himself Sign in the Incarnate One. I hold that "his task was to prepare Israel for the consummation, so fulfilling all promises, prophecies and types."[9] The student of the Jesus of history requires for this assertion the substantial historicity of the Gospels, with notable reference—not least for its "knitting together both the Law and the Prophets with God's self-revelation in Jesus Christ"[10]—to the traditionally accorded primacy of Matthew. I note in particular that the affirmation of Markan priority, which runs counter to the early witnesses (cf. 3.1.2), tends inevitably to the truncation of the Christological narrative.[11]

3.2.2 The Christocentric unity of the Bible licenses the figural exegesis often called "typology," which is the preferred way to read Scripture in the fathers and the liturgies. To understand the events of the history narrated in the Scriptures of Israel as summated in the Messiah Jesus is, even empirically considered, quite as legitimate as the claims to heirship of those Scriptures put forward by rabbinic Jews. Jesus the Christ is, seen retrospectively, the fulfillment of the Jewish hope. And since the Church is Christ's Mystical Body, the figural sequence climaxing in Christ also extends forward into the mysteries of the Church, which are the anticipated presence of his final Parousia. Holding this mode of exegesis to be central, I prize precritical exegesis, though recognizing merit in some practitioners of historical-critical and (other) literary-critical approaches. I accept Henri de Lubac's view that St. John Cassian's fourfold scheme of the senses of Scripture expresses the deep mind of the premodern exegetic tradition,[12] and I defend not only, then, Christological typology ("allegory") but also tropology (cf. 5.4; 5.4.4,) and anagogy (cf. 6.3), as well as the "literal" sense which furnishes the immediately given (and intended) meaning of historical events (in the historical genres of Scripture), cosmic processes (in the sapiential genres), prophetic intimations (in the prophetic genres), and legal enactments (in the forensic genres).

3.3   The Mission of the Messiah

The centering of the biblical revelation in the Incarnation of the Word requires that the Incarnate One be the Messiah of Israel, since the divine promise of a condition of perfect union between man and God is made to Israel as to be achieved through her and thus in her. The particularity of Jesus' mission to Israel does not rule out—rather, it calls for—a universality of effect on humankind at large (cf. 3.1.1), since the point of his mission is salvation in accord with the promise of the Scriptures, that is, by restoring his people and so saving the nations through eschatological assimilation to the vocation of Israel.[13] This will be the ultimate form of life for persons together in the upshot of the historical process. Hence even the biological conception of the Messiah fills the Church with joy. "Today is the beginning of our salvation and the manifestation of the mystery from all eternity: the Son of God becomes the son of the virgin and Gabriel announces the good tidings of grace."[14] The liturgical name for the Messiah's conception, "beginning of our salvation," indicates how human history, the continuation of the development of the cosmos (cf. 2.3.4), starts to reach its final consummation. It is, then, unsurprising that the God-centred angelic powers (cf. 2.4.4) should be coinvolved, suitably accommodated to human understanding. I take "accommodation" to mean, in the excellently chosen words of a literary critic, the way in which "ineffable truths are lowered and the human mind lifted up so that they converge without misrepresentation."[15]

3.3.1 The Messiahship of Jesus is to be understood in terms of the "triple office" of prophet, priest, and king, and this is necessary if the form of sacred society God ushered in through him is fittingly to prepare persons for their final fulfillment. They must be taught the truth of God, shaped liturgically by the worship of God, and brought into a solidarity which reflects at the hypostatic level the ordered beauty of the cosmos. Messiahship is, in respect of the kingly office, of theo-political significance—the New Testament confesses Jesus as the eternal heir to David's throne. But thanks to Jesus' simultaneous occupation of the prophetic and priestly offices, Messiahship is not of theo-political significance alone. Thus, his teaching which declared the promises of God now to be fulfilled in him makes him the final and definitive prophet. His priestly office, moreover, entails his perfecting of Israel's worship, since David's line had fashioned and equipped Israel's true worship in authentic continuation of the work of Moses and Aaron, for Israel's history was to find in her worship its culmination and meaning (cf. 1–2 Chr and Sir 50).[16] The concord between these offices is wonderfully rendered in the incarnate Word in whom prophetic fullness, perfect priesthood, and complete kingship are forever joined.

3.4   *The Mission's Fulfillment*

The point at which the Messianic prophecies converged—
in startling and unforeseeable fashion—appeared only
when Jesus came to fulfill them,[17] not just by his teaching
and authoritative shepherding but also by his Sacrifice,
which itself must be understood latreutically, as a climactic and unsurpassable act of worship—"unsurpassable,"
owing to the identity of the One who made it, and "climactic," since it summed up the filial homage he had paid
throughout his life. I take the interrelated terms "worship," "offering," and "sacrifice" to be the key to the death
of the Messiah as the congruent climax to his life.

> He gave himself completely in his whole life; he did not
> slay himself. But the making of the perfect offering in
> a sinful world inevitably drew down upon itself the con-
> centrated forces of evil in a desperate effort to destroy
> it or mutilate its perfection. The onslaught had to be
> allowed to go to the ultimate point of ferocity, for with-
> out rendering his offering imperfect the Offerer could
> not meet force with force or hate with hate. So the life
> passed through death in a way of which the death of
> the victim in the ancient sacrifices was only the faintest
> and most remote foreshadowing.[18]

God's Messiah offered himself personally in sacrifice as a
sin offering, the true sacrifice of atonement, becoming
thereby the enthroned Priest, the crowned King in heaven
(cf. Heb 2:7, 9). And so, though he died at Passovertide,
it was the sacrifice of Yom Kippur that was fulfilled in his
perfect Oblation.[19]

3.4.1 The upshot of his death was superabundance of
peace between man and God. By the death of Christ, man

is restored to that righteousness originally intended for him but lost in his historical beginnings, and yet no violence is done to the justice and order of God's treatment of creatures. Christ rendered to God the love humanity owed yet withheld. His self-gift to the Father in our name was accepted in an endless outpouring of divine peace, declaring the generosity of God even as it vindicated God's righteousness, since in this wonderful exchange God's "order is preserved through his own assumption of the conditions of estrangement."[20]

3.4.2 Even before his betrayer turned him over to his enemies, Christ had given himself to his disciples "by his own hand,"[21] surrendering himself to them in Bread broken and Wine outpoured. He ensured thereby the meaning of his own Sacrifice, which united in indissoluble fashion philanthropy with theocentricity. The Paschal Mystery has, therefore, its cognate sign in the institution of the Holy Eucharist. The moment of the institution of the chalice is the key epiphany from which not only the title of this systematics in outline but also its theological principle of order (cf. 1.4.1) take their rise. When, in the Cenacle, Christ's blood, in its sacramental sign, was poured into the chalice of the Supper board, the peace of God found its plenary bestowal in the receptacle of the world. "For God was more bounteous in giving Himself so as to make man able to raise himself again than if, simply of Himself, He had pardoned."[22]

3.4.3 The Church's confession of the mystery of the "descent into hell" draws attention to the unlimited character of this self-giving whose effects reach the immortal elements—the "souls"—in the hypostases of the departed.

Indeed, reaction—whether receptive or repulsive—to the One who descended to the depths of the earth (cf. Eph 4:9-10) brings with it the eschatological differentiation of the dead. In climactic divine-human form, Christ's loving "to the end" presents a final choice: the unnatural embrace of nihilism or the loving acceptance of the generosity of being (cf. 6.4.5).

3.4.4 The life of Jesus cannot be understood except in terms of its paschal pathway. His self-giving has its goal in the inauguration of the Kingdom—the judged yet consummated creation and the final outcome of the divine self-disclosure in its saving action. That "inauguration" takes place through his death and Resurrection. The "righteousness-yet-mercy" God disclosed to Israel in the Torah and the Prophets as his own chief identifying marks receive their surpassing expression in the Jesus of the Cross and Resurrection, to which the Jesus of the Transfiguration bore witness in the Passion prediction, on his way to glory (cf. Matt 16:21). "You were transfigured on the Mount, and insofar as they were able, O Lord God, your disciples contemplated your glory, so that seeing you crucified they would understand that you willingly undertook your Passion, and proclaim to the world that truly you are the splendour of the Father."[23] On the basis of the paschal pathway, the divine "righteousness-yet-mercy" can be redescribed. It is, as Balthasar's theological aesthetics bear witness, *endless charity*: "God's own love, the manifestation of which is the manifestation of the glory of God." It is "God's final word about himself—and so about the world."[24]

3.4.5 Maintaining as I do the ample continuity of the Jesus of history with the Jesus of faith—itself a requirement of the ontological realism that alone can sustain this redescription of the identifiers of God—I oppose those who would "protect" the "Christ of faith" from historical criticism through suppressing the earthly sign of his Resurrection that is the empty tomb. "The empty tomb is just what prevents us from placing the heavenly story of the Word side by side with the earthly story of Jesus, and thus compels us to recognize that the Word has really come in the flesh, and that the flesh in its turn is really quickened by the Word."[25] In this sense, the bodily Resurrection plays the same role at the end of the Lord's earthly career as the virginal conception (cf. 3.3) does at its beginning: both signify the way the Incarnation will really transform the cosmic process (cf. 2.3.3–2.3.5).

3.4.6 The death from which the Resurrection frees the manhood of Christ is the form of the mortal human condition as such, of which the separation of soul and body is only, in the course of nature, the biologically final expression. Just so, the "life" the Resurrection communicates is "not the state of man while his soul animates his body . . . [but] the life of God grasping the soul and body, removing them from the misery of the flesh and communicating to them the glory of the Spirit."[26] This is the final transformation offered to persons in the cosmos, the plenary inflow of divine life into the hypostatic order (cf. 2.2.7); hence the prayer of the Church that Christ may find the "flame" of her Easter hope continually "alight, that Morning-Star which knows no setting, which came back from the realm of the dead and shed its clear light upon mankind."[27]

3.4.7 Meanwhile, in the Ascension the New Adam, who was also the bearer of the vocation of Israel, has been led into the presence of the Ancient of Days (cf. Acts 2:32-36), to the throne of the Presence whence the Spirit will go forth. Christ's manhood is exalted not only visibly above the heavens but invisibly over every creature, to the awe of angelic powers (cf. Eph 1:20-22); transforming as it does the creature-Creator relationship, his Ascension necessarily impacts the elements of nonhuman intellectuality in the cosmos (cf. 2.4.4). He becomes not only the Head of his body the Church but Lord of all creation (cf. Eph 1:22-23). The Ascension marks the completion of the movement begun with the Incarnation, for the Logos now leads humanity as a spotless Bride into the Father's house. The Church enjoys a cosmic significance, owing to the reconfiguration of all things round her divine-human Head. "Having accomplished your mission and united things on earth with things in heaven, you ascended into glory, O Christ our God, being nowhere separated from those who love you, but remaining present with us and calling: 'I am with you and no one is against you.' "[28]

3.4.8 Sent by Father and Son, the Holy Spirit at Pentecost causes the renovated creation—which may also be called the ecclesialised cosmos—to spring into being, thus manifesting the hidden mystery of the Church, prepared during the public ministry and born from the Cross in the person of holy Mary, the God-bearer.[29] At Whitsun, the Church is quickened by the Spirit with divine energy, so that the glory in which his manhood now stands arrayed may be communicated to human beings, who are the adopted brethren of the incarnate Word. The Father gives the Spirit to the humanized Son in such a way that the Son may give the Spirit in turn to the Church that is his Body. I appeal here to the graced understanding of the evangelist John, whom the Greek Church calls "the Theologian": " 'Out of his heart shall flow rivers of living water.' Now this he said about the Spirit, which those who believed in him were to receive; for as yet the Spirit had not been given, because Jesus was not yet glorified" (John 7:39).

3.5   *The Divinity of the Sent and Anointed One*

Only the Godhead of the Son gives the work of the Messiah its universal efficacy (cf. 3.1.1; 3.3). Hence I treat the faith of Nicaea as indispensable to the theological enterprise. I am unrepentantly Athanasian and Cyrilline (and therefore Newmanian).[30] The subsisting Word in which the Father expresses himself is personally the sharing of the Father's being. In St. Athanasius's defence of the Creed of Nicaea, "the Son is in the Father . . . because the whole being of the Son is proper to the Father's substance, as radiance from light and a stream from a fountain."[31] The fruitfulness of the Father in the Son testifies to the way his *ousia* is essential love, on which compare 1 John 4:8, "God is love." (Surely this is why St. Thomas added that the Word cannot be uttered in God without "breaking forth in love," that is, producing the Holy Spirit.[32]) I follow the Council of Chalcedon in its teaching on the inseparable but unconfused union of divinity and humanity in the single hypostasis of the Word Incarnate,

> consubstantial with the Father as to divinity, consubstantial with us as to humanity, fashioned as we are, only sinless, begotten of the Father before all ages as to divinity, but in the last days for our sakes and for our

salvation born of the Virgin Mary, Mother of God, as
to humanity—one and the same Christ, Son, Lord,
only-begotten, whom we recognize to be in two natures,
without confusion, without change, without division
or separation, the difference of natures not being re-
moved by their union, but rather the properties of each
of the two natures remaining whole, and meeting in a
single person or hypostasis, not separated or divided
into two Persons, but one and the same Lord Jesus
Christ.[33]

I understand the formula to be primarily a reflection of
the thinking of St. Cyril, albeit with significant touches
from the Tome of Pope St. Leo. I therefore interpret the
Chalcedonian definition as even more strongly a statement of the unity of the Word Incarnate than of the duality
of his modes of being and activity. I hold that the Christology of the Church stresses primarily, then, the one hypostasis who is the eternal Exemplar of all things—and the
means, accordingly, of their return to God—and who in
time, in the humanity he assumed, was born, suffered,
and exalted so as to bring to their Goal in a fashion fitted
to fallen creatures those who had in him their Source.
Thus Bl. John Henry Newman writes of the Son in relation to the universe, "He made Himself its Archetype, and
stamped upon it the image of His own Wisdom. . . . He
was the beginning of the creation of God, in respect of
time, so was He its first principle or idea in respect to
typical order."[34] And again: "Hence it was that He was
fitted, and He alone, to become the First-born of all things,
and to exercise a synkatabasis [condescension] which
would be available for the conservation of the world."[35]
The Son originates that which cosmically mediates his
presence, such that the triune God is immanently present

to the created order in a specifically Christocentric manner, rendering congruent the transformation of the cosmos by the Incarnation and Paschal Mystery. In the words of St. Athanasius: "To change the corruptible to incorruption was proper to none other than the Saviour himself who in the beginning made all things out of nothing; only the Image of the Father could re-create the likeness of that Image in men."[36]

3.5.1 So far as man, made in the divine image, is concerned, it is, then, "theonomy which actually liberates autonomy, and which at the same time defines the content of human autonomy, which is in itself undefined and open."[37] In the words of the Pastoral Constitution on the Church of the Second Vatican Council, so often echoed in the magisterial teaching of Bl. John Paul II, "Christ the new Adam, in the very revelation of the mystery of the Father and of his love, fully reveals man to himself and brings to light his most high calling" (*Gaudium et Spes* 22).[38]

3.5.2 The Son's hypostatic distinctiveness within the eternal Trinity is the key to his re-creating mission by way of sacrifice in time. As the One who is altogether filially responsive to the Father's communication of the divine nature, the Son already, from all eternity, places himself in a posture of sacrifice, such that I would allow the claim of George MacDonald in a rightly celebrated citation: When Christ was crucified, "he did that in the wild weather of his outlying provinces in the torture of the body of his revelation which he had done at home in glory and gladness"[39] (cf. 6.2.4). His temporal mission to a fallen world enabled him to express his hypostatic identity more fully than would have been the case had he, in pursuit of the supernatural elevation of creation, taken to himself the nature of an unfallen species. I echo, therefore, the cry "O happy fault!" of the Easter *Exsultet*, without for all that denying the Incarnation *credo* of St. Maximus: "This is the divine purpose conceived before the beginning of beings. In defining it we say that this mystery is the preconceived goal for which everything exists."[40]

Source: L. Ouspensky and V. Lossky, *The Meaning of Icons* (ET Crestwood, NY: St. Vladimir's Seminary, 1982, 2nd edition), p. 206.

Chapter 4

Tradition as the Transmission of Revelation

Novgorod School, The Descent of the Holy Spirit

The mystery of Pentecost is the completion, in salvation history, of the revelation of the Holy Trinity. The icon of Pentecost thus represents the climax of the Church's foundation on the persons of the apostles at the moment when she begins to unfold her life in the play of charism and office, supported by the grace and truth of the Holy Spirit. The Church, so constituted, carries Tradition in her heart and makes its content manifest in her liturgy. And all this is not for its own sake but for man-in-the-cosmos, who, in this icon, closes the semicircle of the apostles, standing receptive and crowned.

4.1   The Theology of Tradition

The Gospel is not only message; it is, more, the fullness of the self-communication of God to man (cf. *Dei Verbum* 9). The Church is the agent of Tradition, and inasmuch as she is Christ's Mystical Body she is also the content of Tradition: "in her doctrine, life and worship, [the Church] perpetuates and transmits to every generation all that she herself is, all that she believes" (*Dei Verbum* 8). Since she is the Mystical Body of the Trinitarian Son who acted through his life, death, and Resurrection to bring her into being, endowed with all her capacities for manifesting the inauguration of the Kingdom—"she is, on earth, the seed and the beginning of that kingdom" (*Lumen Gentium* 5)—she cannot name herself without simultaneously naming these further realities: Christ and his great mysteries as reproduced in the lesser mysteries of her life and worship.

4.1.1 The gift of these realities is inseparable from their intelligible mediation—just as the revelation that takes place through embodiment in the key biblical episodes cannot be fully constituted without its accompaniment by exhibition in language of the meaning of these events (cf. 5.1). If charity, being love, casts us upon reality just as it is in sheer simplicity, faith, being knowledge, reaches reality only by means of judgments to which interior assent is required, and these judgments are communicable articulations concerning God and the plans of his heart: "the eternal purpose which he has realized in Christ Jesus our Lord" (Eph 3:11), the "plan of the mystery hidden for ages in God who created all things" (Eph 3:9). The passing on of Tradition includes, therefore, the passing on of fitting language about its content, and it is this language—not

Tradition itself—which "develops," in so doing not *changing* apostolic truth as consciously entertained by the mind of the Church but *amplifying its expression*. Postapostolically, the Spirit's assistance is given to the Church not only that she may guard the apostolic deposit but also that she may make it bear fruit in minds and hearts. This happens not least when what was contained in the deposit preconceptually, obscurely, in an unformulated state, becomes at last explicit to illumine minds and rejoice hearts that know the supreme Truth to be also the highest Good. I am inclined to prefer the term "unfolding" to "developing," since what is expressed is not so much new truths but the depth, richness, and many-sidedness of the truth revealed once and for all in the incarnate Word in his recentering of Scripture and all creation in his multiple relations with the world. The understanding enjoyed by the apostles through the prophetic light received from Christ and, in overflowing measure, from his Spirit at Pentecost has an unsurpassable dignity, which the Church underlines by taking revelation—the object of Catholic faith—to be "completed with the apostles."[1] It is the task of all subsequent comprehension to aim, asymptotically, at the apostolic measure. "Therefore let the understanding, the knowledge, the wisdom . . . of the whole Church grow and advance with the advance of the ages, but . . . in the same teaching, the same meaning, the same truth"[2] (cf. 3.1.7).

4.1.2 I stress with Bl. John Henry Newman the importance of "ethos," or moral temper, in disposition toward Tradition. As the fathers of the Oxford Movement saw, if the demands of revelation are to be responded to aright, there must be openness to God by humility of mind and heart and the generosity of spirit that is capable of following a great ideal.[3] A rightly disposed heart preserves the vision of its object and acts as the safeguard of faith, protecting it against the extremes of reductionism and superstition.

4.1.3 With Hans Urs von Balthasar, I find the mystery aspect of the revelation-in-transmission that is Tradition—a trait signifying not deficiency of meaning but a superabundance thereof—to be best expressed through the combining of abstractly conceptual with concretely imagistic description.[4] The uniqueness and personally self-involving character of the divine action, grounding as it does the mysteric in Tradition (cf. 4.1), points to a primacy for metaphorical description over conceptual. Yet the intelligibility of the declarations which accompany and interpret the divine action and which are passed down as such, and further refined, in the Church's traditioning process (cf. 4.1.1) counterindicates a primacy for conceptual description over imagistic. A corrective complementarity of the two is called for within a wider acknowledgement that the *event* of revelation is precisely disclosure, and thus chiefly cataphatic, while the overflowing plenitude of the *content* thus disclosed calls for an apophatic check on cataphasis. And this, of its own nature, issues in adoration and praise: "O the depth of the riches and wisdom and knowledge of God!" (Rom 11:33). Habitual tact for combining cataphasis and apophasis also belongs with "proper ethos" (cf. 4.1.2) in approaching Tradition.

4.1.4 Tradition does not merely furnish certain oral traditions supplementary to Scripture but, in its wholeness, envelops Scripture, since it bears within it the principles that enable the right interpretation of the Bible, and makes it possible for the faithful to live out in a right spirit the comprehensive divine plan. Hence I agree with my confrère, the late Cardinal Yves Congar, that "Tradition creates a totality, a harmony, a synthesis."[5] In this, the notion of Tradition enjoys an affinity with the idea of systematics. While combining reason in its overall purview with the (even) larger space of sacral thinking (cf. 1.2.1; 1.3), systematics is not least the attempt theoretically to render in theological writing that which is given in the total awareness of revelation available through a variety of media (scriptural texts, liturgical gestures and texts, holy images, doctrinal determinations of those in the apostolic succession, and existential living out of the faith in Christian households and monasteries—supremely, by the saints) in the corporate mind of the Church.

4.2   *An Ecclesiology*

I define the Church as the community that carries Tradition, understood as revelation in its transmission over time (cf. 4.1.3). Even before she put forth her formal Creeds, the Church knew the treasure she bore by tacit reference to the *regula fidei*, which is her recognition of the "intrinsic shape and pattern of the revelation itself"[6] (cf. 4.1.4). With Henri de Lubac, I hold faith to be "ecclesial in its mode," albeit "theological [*théologale*] in its object and principle."[7] The guardianship and transmittal of the *Paradosis*—that which is "handed on"—rests with the apostolic Church and notably with its episcopal members; the Byzantine office for the consecration of a bishop asks appropriately that he be a "leader of the blind, a light in darkness, an instructor of the foolish, a teacher of babes, a lamp in the world." This teaching role is inseparable from the other tasks which the ancient author Hippolytus ascribes to the bishop in his treatise *The Apostolic Tradition*: to be the good shepherd of God's holy flock and high priest after the order of Melchizedek, propitiating God by the offering of the Church's eucharistic sacrifice.[8] The bishop stands for God to the Church and for the Church to God, but he does so within the hierarchical communion that joins him to his brothers in the episcopate "under and with Peter."

4.2.1 I am, then, as the reference to "Peter" as a present-day figure suggests, unashamedly Roman in my ecclesiastical allegiance. Without a global primacy, the episcopal principle readily becomes dysfunctional, as the doctrinal difficulties of Anglicans and the jurisdictional disputes of the Orthodox attest. I regard the Pope of Rome as the shepherd par excellence of the universal Church, bearing in mind the words of St. Leo:

> Each bishop has a special care for his own flock, and each will have to render an account of the sheep committed to him. But we, for our part, have a care in common with them all, and the ministry of each one of them is a part of ours. And when, from all over the world, recourse is had to the seat of the blessed apostle Peter, and in our intervention is sought that love for the universal Church which the Lord laid upon him as a duty, we feel the weight of our charge to be so much the heavier as our debt to all is the greater.[9]

Such a primacy is appropriate to the age of the Holy Spirit and the risen Lord: I note with Charles Journet that the "supreme unity of the Holy Spirit, as also the unity of the glorified Christ, both hidden from our eyes, must be externally expressed, so that their single voice may be audible to the senses of men," while no clearer "sacrament" of their sovereign invisible authority could be found than by "investing with the supreme visible jurisdiction a single head who should gather all the Church around himself."[10] I can say, therefore, with Newman, "What a bishop is to his Church—such [is] the Pope to all the bishops and the whole Church."[11] I hold that this Western, Latin, Roman affirmation can readily be translated into an Eastern, Byzantine, Greek version of itself: the bishop of Rome, considered as the *prôtos*, the first among bishops, has a responsibility for the functioning of the entire episcopal *taxis* and thus for the life of all the churches of God.

4.2.2 I do not, however, prefer hierarchology to an ecclesiology of the whole Church—precisely because we cannot set these magnitudes against each other. I hold the Church to be a communion reflecting the unity of the triune Persons (in the Cyprianic accents of the Second Vatican Council, "a people brought to unity from the unity of the Father, the Son and the Holy Spirit"[12]), but the *life* of the Church communion is that of the Mystical Body of Christ which includes not only the hierarchical orders of bishops, presbyters, and deacons but a vast array of complementary charismata among the lay faithful (including nonordained monastics). Their orchestration belongs to the work of the third Trinitarian person in his role as the perfect Unifier (cf. 6.2.6). The Holy Spirit, agent of the union of the divine and human natures in Christ (cf. Luke 1:35), is also the agent of our union with Christ, making us, in the variety of tasks within the Church communion, one Body with Christ, "as it were one mystical person."[13] Before the coming of the Spirit, Christ's followers were connected by discipleship; after that coming, they are joined by an inward Principle, animated by the same life into which people are initiated by the baptismal mystery, in which there is no difference between membership of the Church and membership of Christ—so long as the robe of new baptismal righteousness be not cast off.

4.2.3 Baptismal initiation, so I maintain, admits not into the particular church but the universal Church, for the particular church is "really but a fragment of it, as being that part of it which is seen and can be pointed out, and as resembling in type, and witnessing it, and leading towards it,"[14] while the universal Church, the mother of our new birth, is the heavenly Jerusalem on earth (cf. Gal 4:26). The particular church has no life except insofar as it is part of the Church universal and as the latter is present and active in it. I hold to the organic unity of particular churches in the Catholic Church, which has as its precondition a transcendental factor: the ontological and temporal anteriority of the Church herself, born from the side of Christ on the Cross and manifested in the Cenacle, to each individual, particular church.[15]

> Without subsisting in the manner of a Platonic "idea," she is for all that more than a mere aggregate [of communities or persons, q.v.]. The divine call that summons her into reality and the divine principle which animates her make her always anterior and superior to anything which can be enumerated and distinguished in her; you can say that she was born of the Apostles, yet they themselves were first conceived by her. And it is this Church in her entirety who is, in her unicity and her unity, in-

dissolubly a hierarchical society and a community of grace, under two different aspects respectively.[16]

4.2.4 I admit that the proper polyphony of catholicity can be overborne by ecclesial homogenization. But I see this as a failure of Christian imagination, to be overcome by a more informed awareness of the many expressive forms orthodoxy can take as both cultus and theology, and not as a ground for rejecting universal primacy. A particular patrimonial tradition of worship and thought, if it is sound, illustratively embodies the *Paradosis* and does not seek to erect over against the norms of Tradition a court of appeal of its own. I have already committed myself to the duality of Western and Eastern liturgical inspiration (cf. introduction) and to a (pre-eschatological) plurality of theologies in the service of the single faith (cf. 1.1.4; 1.1.3). In the case of my own country, I desiderate for the Church of the Roman Rite a distinctive form of Latin Christianity that accords with its corporate story: a form influenced by the liturgical history and customs, the saints and spiritual writers, the art and literature of the mediaeval English people and their recusant successors (to which must be added the Catholic elements in the post-Reformation Anglican patrimony through the accession to our Church of the Ordinariate of Our Lady of Walsingham)—and, mutatis mutandis, I expect the same for any *ethnos* that endures through historic time.

4.2.5 I eschew excessive stress on the Church's pilgrim nature as generative of ecclesiological ephemeralism. I regard the loss of Christian memory as the chief reason for diminution of the Church in the estimation of her members.

4.3 *The Sacred Liturgy and Tradition*

Not only is the liturgical sacramentality of the Church the means whereby she grows in her organically constituted unity, adding to it fresh members, it is also the medium for the reception of Tradition at its most comprehensive and intimately engaging of persons. I hold that the sacred liturgy, with its proper extension in iconography, is the best teacher of the ensemble of attitudes that right ethos should compose. The liturgy's valued role vis-à-vis human subjectivity complements its invaluable role vis-à-vis divine objectivity in the continuing celebration of Christ's mysteries, which thereby become accessible in the sacramental life pursued through the Church's year. This is how I understand the dictum of Dom Prosper Guéranger of Solesmes: "The liturgy is tradition itself, at its highest power and solemnity."[17] In celebrating the liturgy, the Church resumes the triple office of her Lord (cf. 3.3.1): she participates in the worship the incarnate Son offers the Father (the priestly office); she proclaims God's wonderful works (the prophetic office); she furthers the establishment of the Kingdom (the regal office) by inviting persons to enter the new creation.

4.3.1 Just as the liturgy is normally epicletic, invoking the Holy Spirit to attain its ends (from the special epiclesis to the Spirit in the eucharistic rites of the East we see how, in the Roman liturgy too, the Anaphora's epicletic quality enables the words of institution to exercise their efficacy), so likewise is Tradition at large, for the Holy Spirit is Tradition's transcendent Subject. It is through the Spirit that the risen Lord continues to give himself actively to the Church (cf. 3.4.7–3.4.8). The passionate love of the Father for human beings (cf. John 3:16), reaching its climax in the Passion of his Son, is henceforth poured out by his Spirit in the Church, the Son's Body. "Now, in the last times, all the torrents of love that pour from the Spirit of Jesus flow together in the great river of life that is the liturgy."[18]

4.3.2   It is through the Spirit that Tradition points forward to the End, since, as the outpouring of the triune life, the Spirit is the eschatological Gift (cf. 6.3; 6.4.3). He it is who makes possible the transition from Alpha to Omega—from the Word who, as the Beginning, inaugurates both creation and (as incarnate) salvation, to the same Word, now not only humanized but transfigured in glory, as the Omega point of a world redeemed. The more deeply we immerse ourselves in Tradition, the more we are borne forward toward the promised fullness of God. As "the holy ark containing sacred tradition at its most intense,"[19] the Church's worship is a foretaste of the heavenly liturgy (cf. *Sacrosanctum Concilium* 8), and this is most readily seen, we consider, in the Church of the Byzantine Rite. It is the liturgy that sustains the eschatological orientation of Tradition to the future when its content will be laid bare in the open vision of God, with the definitive transformation of persons in enjoyment of the supreme Good (cf. 6.4.3). The theologian must be steeped in the ambience of liturgical prayer, celebrated according to the mind of the Church as steward of the mysteries, if he is to keep habitually in mind the final outcome of the revelation he serves, without which the chalice of God will not be filled.

Source: A. Grabar, *Byzantine Painting* (ET Geneva: Skira, 1953), p. 140.

Chapter 5

The Mysteric Pattern of Christian Existence

Serbian School, St. Basil Celebrating the Holy Mysteries
St. Sophia's, Ochrid

The transposition of the greater mysteries of Christ into the lesser mysteries of the life of the Church is shown most graphically at the eucharistic altar. Here, supremely, the Christ who is the origin of the entire sacramental economy communicates to his brethren the grace and power of his saving deeds, summed up in his death and Resurrection. From this radiant centre all the pathways of the Christian life open out in virtue and holiness, following the example of the saints. What grace entails for sinful human beings here becomes perspicuous, in repair of what is wounded in human nature and for the sake of its wonderful deification. A new direction is conferred on society, culture, and the movement of history as a whole.

5.1   *Revelation and the Greater Mysteries*

Revelation occurs through epiphanic episodes in the cosmic and historical orders, episodes accompanied by an exposition in language of their meaning (cf. 4.1.1). It takes the form of the provision of interpreted signs in which God acts as transcendent cause to point to the meaning he intends. As the French philosopher of religion Maurice Blondel insisted, the sign "can 'offer the infinite only under the guise of the finite,' [and yet]" to those who are well-disposed toward or receptive of the infinite within themselves, it is a sign that is welcome" (cf. 4.1.2); contrastingly: "to those who are not so disposed, but are more inclined to be self-sufficient or satisfied with something in the natural order, it is a sign of irritation to be repelled. 'That is why what subdues and illumines some is also what hardens and blinds others. *Signum contradictionis.*'"[1] Of these epiphanic episodes, the most crucial are the chief signs found in the career of the Word Incarnate to whose person the description "sign of contradiction," *sêmeion antilegomenon* (Luke 2:34), was applied prophetically by the holy man Simeon at the worshiping heart of Israel, the Jerusalem Temple. They constitute the maximally dense self-disclosure of God, impacting for the sake of salvation the minds and hearts of those who apprehend them. As the presence of the reality of God, humanly embodied, Christ, the Sign of God par excellence (cf. 3.2.1), discloses the logic of God's intention in acting in the world. My theology is necessarily a semiology, because the plenitude of God's presence to persons in creation is, since the moment of Adam's sin, a fullness of occluded presence, which requires signalization to become effective in human existence. It is in the signs that are the mysteries of Christ's life that God gives himself to be known and loved, thereby drawing persons transformatively into the ambit of the triune exchange (cf. 3.4–3.4.7).

5.1.1   Christ is in his own person the origin of the entire sacramental economy. His is the originating sacramentality, constituted permanently in fullness in him (cf. 3.2.1); that of the sacraments is a derived sacramentality, which is received and always radically dependent. By the Holy Spirit he reactualises his saving deeds through the symbolism of the sacraments.[2]

5.2   The Drama of the Greater Mysteries as the Archetype of Christian Existence

I maintain that since Christians form with Christ one Mystical Body of which he is the Head,[3] all his saving acts in all of their aspects can apply to men. In the words of Bl. Columba Marmion,

> What makes the mysteries of Jesus ours is, above all, that the Eternal Father saw us when seeing His Son in each one of the mysteries Jesus lived, and that Christ accomplished them as head of the Church. Because of that, I will even say that the mysteries of Christ are more our mysteries than they are His. Christ, inasmuch as He is the Son of God, would not have had to submit to the humiliations of the Incarnation, the suffering and pain of the Passion; He would have had no need of the triumph of the resurrection that followed the ignominy of His death. He went through all that as head of the Church; He took upon himself *our* miseries and *our* weaknesses: "He has borne *our* infirmities." He willed to tread the road that we have to tread ourselves, and

He merited for us, as our head, the grace to walk where
He walked in each one of his mysteries.[4]

5.2.1 I agree with Balthasar in his theological dramatics
that the "hour" of Jesus' death and Resurrection must be
transposed into the postpaschal life of the faithful, for which
it provides the crucial form.[5] The premier instantiation of
this truth is the destiny of the Mother of the Lord. Standing
by the Cross of Jesus, as the Daughter of Zion par excellence, to ratify his once-for-all Oblation, she became, as
Helpmate of the Redeemer, the first to enter body and soul
into glory, the woman "clothed with the sun" showed in
vision to St. John (Rev 12:1). But I add with St. Thomas
that all the mysteries of the life of Christ enjoy exemplary
causality vis-à-vis Christian existence—though, to be sure,
the remaining "greater mysteries" are ordered to the *mysterium paschale*, this greatest mystery of them all. The
"hour" makes sense of the life of the Incarnate One in its
totality. As the letters of St. Paul demonstrate, Christians
accept that Paschal Mystery as establishing the rhythm of
human existence for the future: "If we have been united
with him in a death like his, we shall certainly be united
with him in a resurrection like his" (Rom 6:5). The transposition from Christ to disciples—sacramentally, from the
greater mysteries to the lesser—brings fruitfulness in mission and in mystical holiness. Thus does the Holy Spirit
open up endless possibilities which issue from the form of
the sacrificial existence of the Son.

5.2.2 The mysteries of Christ's humiliation—I mean,
above all, his Passion—are the meritorious cause of his
Resurrection, Ascension, and Session on the Father's
right. In meriting his own Resurrection he was meriting

the resurrection of the members of his Mystical Body. His vast suffering, lived out through charity by One who was divine, showed greater love than was needed to atone (cf. 3.4.1). The lavish excess of the Sacrifice entailed for his humankind, not only repair, but innovation (cf. 2.3.4), applied to men through their union in the Mystical Body. The Father's good pleasure at the Sacrifice of the Son, his delight made manifest in the Resurrection, was simultaneously the declaration of the world's salvation.

5.2.3 I hold, accordingly, the mysteries of Christ's glorification to be the exemplary cause of the fulfillment of the existence of human persons in God, which is our final transformation. The mystery of the Sacrifice, understood as offered by Son to Father in the Spirit, does not yet suffice for the communication of its own merits. I note with Newman, "On the Cross, while in the tomb, while in hell, the treasure existed, the precious gift was perfected, but it lay hid, it was not yet available for its gracious ends; it was not diffused, communicated, shared in, enjoyed."[6] The Ascension is the Christological epiclesis to which Pentecost answers; the Holy Spirit is sent in order to configure the Church to Christ. The glorification in the Spirit of the humanized eternal Son constitutes the Church in her means and continuing cause, enabling her members to be united with the sacred humanity of Christ by the action of the Holy Spirit who indwells in them to make them one Body (cf. 3.4.6; 4.3.1).

5.2.4 In fine: the Paschal Mystery is a mystery of saving worship where the Son in his Sacrifice sums up the mission expressed in his Incarnation and public ministry by a supreme act of praise of the Father, which is also his effective pleading with the Father for the grace of redemption for the world.[7] His death is a sacrifice of praise that is also a sacrifice of impetration and, as such, was accepted by the Father when he raised Jesus Christ from the dead and exalted him to his right hand. This accepted Sacrifice of the Cross was rendered salvifically effective for others when the glorified Lord became at Pentecost coprinciple with the Father of the Holy Spirit in his coming forth in time from Father and Son. But precisely because the Paschal Mystery is in this way a mystery of saving worship, it can also be the source from which there issues the sacramental life of the Church.

5.3   The Sacraments as the Lesser Mysteries

I hold that the sacraments are precisely acts of praise and pleading carried out on the basis of the Paschal Mystery. The missions of Son and Spirit make it possible in the sacramental economy of the Church for the same salvific worship Jesus offered in his death and Resurrection to have its scope extended to us, so that the grace the triune God bestowed on Jesus as predestined Head of a redeemed humanity comes to affect also his members (cf. 5.2.2). The sacraments constitute a transposition of the greater mysteries, those of Christ's life, death, and Resurrection, into cultic acts which reorient existence, inserting it into the sphere of the Trinitarian embrace. The divine power unites human beings to Christ through faith and the sacraments of faith, assimilating them to Christ in his saving deeds. By taking up earthly realities into his glorified saving activity, his invisible heavenly action becomes visible in these signs. The ritual dramas of the sacramental actions "mimic" various aspects of the saving acts of God in Christ—they use symbolic representations of those acts. But they are not only mimesis, since the risen Christ by his divine power reactualises the redemptive acts he carried out in his humanity for our salvation and makes the sacramental actions the prolongation of those same saving acts—above all, of his life-giving death (cf. 3.4–3.4.1). The historical mysteries of Christ are the direct causes of the grace they have merited and which is given in the sacraments. The interior act of worship which made them saving mysteries endlessly endures in the glorified Christ. The exterior aspect of the mysteries was the way—the "paschal pathway" (cf. 3.4.4)—through which his glorified humanity was constituted an instrument to bring men salvation. In the lesser mysteries of the sacraments, divine agency can work, therefore, from time-bound events as from a model, thanks to the boundless spiritual power contained in the greater mysteries of the original events. I thus recognize the relation between the greater mysteries and the lesser to be one of both efficacious and exemplary causality. The divine Agent, working through the instrument that is Christ in his mysteries, produces in human beings a likeness to that model. In the words of St. Thomas, "both the Passion and the Resurrection are the cause of justification,"[8] the Passion by removing evils in us, the Resurrection by beginning in us the ultimate good things.[9] The fruiting in us of the Paschal Mystery as the transformation of sinful creatures is, Thomas says, a twofold mystery at work by a duality of causal paths.

5.3.1 By inaugurating or enhancing a God-given disposition in us and assisting us with "actual" or momentary graces appropriate to the form of our life-situation, each sacrament gives grace in its own proper fashion, the nature of which is specified by its particular liturgy. I hold that each sacrament unites the recipient in a special way to Christ in his Mystical Body by allowing the recipient to enter into some aspect of the mystery of the Church as God in Christ through his Spirit acts in and through her for the goals of his saving plan. Thus in *Baptism* Christians appropriate the Church's filial nature—through assimilation to Christ, whose Bride she has become—as child of the Father, and in *Confirmation* that same nature is now strengthened with the Pentecostal power the Spirit of the Son bestows. In the *Eucharist*, they enter into the mystery of her union with Christ's Sacrifice; in *Penance*, into her enjoyment of the mercy won by Christ on the Cross; and in the *Anointing of the Sick*, into the Church's receiving from God the salvation that, through the Resurrection, conquers physical death. In *Orders* candidates among the baptized who are in the same gender as the Word Incarnate are inducted into the way the Church mediates these gifts by the hands of the ministerial priesthood, the living signs of the Great High Priest in his Headship of the Church, while in *Matrimony*, sacramental marriage, men and women make their own the transformation of the natural marriage covenant in the Church's own nuptial relation with Christ.[10] All this is in its various modes the presence of his saving action, following the word spoken to Mother Julian of Norwich: "All the health and life of the sacraments, all the power and grace of my word, all the goodness which is ordained in Holy Church for you, I am He."[11]

5.3.2 The Church's year, in which the sacraments are contextualized and (in the Byzantine Rite) the icons serially displayed, I take to be the epitome of Christ's paschal pathway, from Incarnation through the drama of his earthly life, via death and Resurrection to return to the Father with his glorified humanity in the Ascension, so as to send the Spirit in preparation for his Parousia to consummate all things (cf. 3.3–3.4.8; 5.2–5.2.4). Meanwhile, the sacramental and liturgical life at large reveals his eschatological abiding through and with the Holy Spirit in the Church (cf. 4.3.1–4.3.2; 5.2.3).

5.3.3 Baptism and the Holy Eucharist are the real entry of persons in every generation into the sacrificial drama of Passion and Resurrection (cf. 5.3). Salvation requires identification with these events, and it takes place as their effect. Initiation into the novel race of Christians, the new people of God, is not now, as in Israel of old, by circumcision, because the fulfillment of the Messiah's own circumcision was the putting off of his whole body in the covenant-creating death of the Cross (cf. Col 2:11). Ecclesial initiation is realized in human beings by the mystery of Holy Baptism, which regenerates through that ultimate circumcision. Death to an old identity takes place through union with the death and entombment of Christ. "You were buried with him in baptism, in which also you were raised with him through faith in the working of God, who raised him from the dead" (Col 2:12). Likewise, then, persons' coming to new life takes place through union with Christ's own rising. Since the Holy Eucharist is the sacramental form of the Sacrifice of Christ on the Cross (not to be separated from his Resurrection and Ascension, the signs of the Oblation's Fatherly acceptance [cf. 5.2.2–5.2.3]), the Mass makes present the reality of which baptismal grace is the fruit, doing so for the sake of fullness in salvific good. According to St. Cyril's teaching, "Participation of the sacred Mysteries is therefore a true and certain confession and commemoration that the Lord is dead and rose for us, besides which we are filled with the divine blessing."[12] The Mass is the sacrifice-banquet of the new covenant, participation in which crowns the faith of Baptism.

5.3.4 I hold that worship is centred not only on Calvary and encounter with the Risen One but on Christ's *transitus* to the Father. The Ascension of the Lord introduces a note of longing expectation into our worship, for it turns our attention away from exclusive concern with past and present (cf. 4.3.2). "Since Jesus is with the Father, none can say where he is according to the canons and criteria of man. But for the same reason—that he is in fact with the Father—it has become possible for human beings to give their answer by being relocated, sacramentally, at the point of turning from the putative kingdoms of man to the messianic Kingdom of God."[13] Covenant history has reached its goal even though world history is still continuing, and in the space between the two the Church of the Holy Eucharist takes up her stance. I note how, in the Church of the Byzantine Rite, the faithful, when attending the Divine Liturgy, stand facing the iconostasis: a sign that their Passover into heaven is accomplished through the incarnate Christ in his advent and in his Ascension. His icon, together with those of the Mother of God, the Forerunner, and the saints, dominates the icon screen, which marks at once the distinction and the connexion between the sanctuary and the *naos* and thus, symbolically, between the Age to Come and the time in which the faithful live now. For the Latin Church, I applaud the rite of eucharistic exposition and adoration, which is the action of the Mass held in contemplation; its heart is the promise of Christ, fulfilled in this "blessed" sacrament, to remain with the Church till the end of the world (cf. Matt 28:20). Like the Buddhist mandala, the eucharistic monstrance is a geometric configuration focusing our attention on the centre. That centre is, however, a radiant hole—it gives access to the universe of the End.

5.3.5   The sacramental life is the sealing of a life in the covenant (cf. 3.1.6), for which the traditional Catholic term is "character." In the words of Matthias Joseph Scheeben, "When we call [character] sacramental, that is not simply because it is conferred by certain sacraments but also because, in the case of those sacraments that confer it, it is the centre of their efficacy and their significance, and in the case of the others it is the basis and ground of their activity."[14]

5.4 Christian Morality as Mystical Tropology

I understand *morality* from the starting point of the transposition of the mysteries and its implications for existence. Theological ethics is a transfiguration of natural ethics into the form of the crucified yet glorious humanity of the Son of God, who is himself the New Adam, the remaking of the human race. In moral doctrine, I seek to integrate the insights of good pagans into an interpretation of the Scriptures that proceeds "tropologically" (cf. 3.2.2): in terms of the behaviour that belongs with the Christ life as ordered to the end of human persons in God.[15] I recall the exhortation to the baptized of our father among the saints, Peter Chrysologus of Ravenna, reiterated in the Roman Liturgy of the Hours: "Now reborn after the pattern of our Lord, let us bear the full and complete image of our maker: not in majesty, in which he is alone, but in innocence, simplicity, meekness, patience, humility, mercy and concord—in which he deigned to become and to be one with us."[16]

5.4.1 My ethics is, then, unashamedly theological, by which I mean, in this context, God-centred. *Beatitude in God* is the real foundation of morality. More exactly: the last end of man is God, while our beatitude is the blossoming—the French have a word for it, *épanouissement*—that results from our union with him. "Thomist morality is not a morality of self-fulfillment; it is a morality of the return of man to God, his last end"[17] (cf. 2.4.7). I concur therefore with Etienne Gilson: although Christian moralists have "regarded the soul of a just man as beautiful and worthy of honour because virtuous," virtue is "itself honourable only because it leads man to God. It is not the supreme good, the *nec plus ultra* that it was to the Greeks, the all-sufficient unconditioned condition of all morality."[18] Nor should beauty of soul be understood in a way that prescinds from Christology; theological ethics cannot be detached from the history of revelation in its Christocentrically determined course, nor natural ethics made extrinsic to the grace that issues from the New Adam (cf. 5.4). The ultimate framework for ethics is the divine desire for the integration of all creation into the blessedness of God's own triune exchange,[19] for which the transposition of the mysteries is the covenanted means.

5.4.2 I applaud the recovery of virtue ethics, for the virtues grant coherence to our actions, allowing us to act well in immediate fashion and to accomplish our good acts with joy. Still, I do not regard an ethics of virtue as an *alternative* to an ethics of precept, which in the Christian dispensation includes not only commands of the natural law but precepts of the covenant renewed in the blood of Christ and the gift of the Spirit.[20] "If you love me, you will keep my commandments" (John 14:15). There can in any case be no contradiction between virtues and precepts, since following the commandments fosters virtue.[21] And yet without prior reference to the virtues—in a kind of preamble to the precepts—we do not know the mode in which the commandments of God are to be followed, which is knowingly, joyfully, and firmly (a person can keep some of the commandments without being in a state of grace, but hardly, insofar as the precepts are ordered to the love of God).[22]

5.4.3 I note that vis-à-vis the cardinal virtues—prudence as the virtue of reason, fortitude as the virtue of the spirited part of the soul, temperance as the virtue of desiring, and justice as the virtue that is in place when all function well and desire and will follow reason's lead—the theological virtues of faith, hope, and charity have primacy. Though the cardinal virtues are lamps that light human existence, they are outshone by these other stars. Thus in the *Purgatorio* the Dante character is struck by the way these new luminaries put the ancient virtues into the shade. As Dante looks into the (symbolic) heavens, Virgil enquires of him, "What is it you're looking at, my son?" And Dante replies, "At those / three lamps whose brilliance makes the pole all burn / Here in the south." Virgil explains, "The four / bright stars you saw this morning now have set, / and these have risen to where those were before."[23] Faith, hope, and charity perfect reason, desire, and will, while justice is now, in the new dispensation, transformed by mercy.

5.4.4 In the final analysis, however, charity alone can constitute a fully moral act, for the other virtues aim at helping to assure the loving gift of self to God and to the neighbour (that he or she may be in God), whilst the natural law and the precepts of the new covenant express diverse conditions without which charity could not be authentic. A good act is one that moves toward the absolute Good, both in God himself and in his created participations, and hence toward that same Good in the neighbour and in myself. "Mystical tropology," the drawing of a Catholic ethics from Scripture, entails a reading which encourages charity to flourish.[24] This was St. Augustine's favoured hermeneutic in *On Christian Doctrine*.[25]

5.4.5 I reject accordingly, as irreconcilable with the Gospel, the Liberalism which conceives moral agency in primarily negative terms as freedom of choice, which might also be described as *amoral autonomy*. Noninterference with the choices of autonomous persons may facilitate freedom insofar as such noninterference may remove obstacles to human flourishing, but noninterference is not of itself freedom, for the latter cannot be had without positive relation to what is good and true. When it is adopted as the first principle of morality, Liberalism, so understood, undermines other claims to the good, such that the individual's act of choosing becomes all that matters, and indifference follows necessarily. In T. S. Eliot's words, "It is a movement not so much defined by its end, as by its starting point; away from, rather than towards, something definite."[26] I note how, contradictorily, Liberal societies often interfere with freely chosen behaviour they consider discriminary; freedom understood as noninterference is not, it seems, a realizable goal even for Liberals. I hold that *proper* autonomy is freedom of choice exercised *toward an objective good*. I deplore the liberty that has lost its connexion with the truth, that is, with the ontological order. Though the will is not drawn in a necessary fashion toward limited goods, and this is why the intellect plays a sometimes disastrous part in judging to do this or that,[27] nonetheless the will desires only those things that are true goods for man. The ability to sin is no essential feature of free will.[28] Were it so, the blessed, supremely free with the freedom of the children of God, would instead be held in bondage.

5.4.6 Since divine revelation proclaims the life humans ought to live as a cruciform life in Christ that leads to glory (the message of the Beatitudes, Matt 5:3-12 [cf. 5.2.1]), with a congruent set of precepts and virtues underpinned by grace (cf. 5.4.2–5.4.4), it enters inevitably into conflict with Liberalism. The tension between a Liberal culture and divine revelation can be expected to arise in a trio of areas: the polis (since negative freedom declares for merely procedural, rather than substantive, norms of civil society), the household (since negative freedom allows in principle for any form of sexual arrangement, according to [adult] choice), and the definition of the beginning and end of life (since negative freedom cannot accept the moral status as persons of those not yet [abortion] or no longer [euthanasia] conscious enough to make choices). These correspond to the areas of "special morals" most studied in the modern era of the Church: the ethics of justice, sexual ethics, and bioethics. In each case, the *sensus fidei* is to be found in those least affected by Liberalism: those Catholic Christians who, well-instructed in their faith in other respects (without which they cannot be numbered among the *fideles*), seek to make the life of the civil realm publicly open to God; have a connatural understanding of the nuptial complementarity of the sexes and the intrinsic symbolism by which conjugal activity entails the bestowal on each partner of all the other is, including fertility; and recognize the inclusion in the hypostatic order of every human being, from conception to the grave.

5.4.7 As these animadversions on contemporary culture ("Liberalism") indicate, I do not believe the imperative to render "encyclopaedically" the union of reason and sacral thinking (cf. 1.2–1.2.1; 1.4) should count as dispensing the systematician from attention to his or her time and place. The organic whole of Christian wisdom is always presented within a particular apostolic and pastoral conjuncture that either helps or hinders the hearing of the Gospel in whose service systematics offers its "roundedly" coherent reflection. This is how I should wish to understand the application to ecclesial practice of the dominical phrase "the signs of the times," much abused as it has been since the Second Vatican Council in forwarding the erroneous maxim "The world sets the agenda."

5.5   Coinherence in the Mysteries: The Mother of God and the Communion of Saints

The life that seeks the supreme Good, having as its context the transposition of the greater mysteries of Christ's life, death, and Resurrection into the lesser mysteries of the Church's liturgical round, is alien to individualism, knowing no person alone but all persons in the communion of saints. I applaud the way that, at the *prothêsis*, the Byzantine liturgy of the Eucharist places on the *discos*, alongside the "holy Lamb,"[29] particles of the sacrificial bread in honour of the saints, as well as in intercession for the living and the dead. I consider the notion of the communion of saints closely bound up with the doctrine and practice of participation in the holy Gifts, as the useful ambiguity of the Latin phrase *communio sanctorum* signals. I take the liturgy to be in consequence the principal ambience of Christian prayer, since the Head is never separable now from his Mystical Body. I therefore understand *personal* prayer to be an interiorized liturgy, offered in the selfsame modes as liturgical worship, namely, adoration, contrition, thanksgiving, and supplication.

5.5.1 Though the basis of such coinherence is God in Christ, its centre is the Mother of the Lord who is also Mother of the Church. Contemplating her is perfect guidance for looking to the Father's Only-Begotten in the Holy Spirit. "Here is the rose wherein the Word divine / was made incarnate."[30] The Latin Church's application to Mary of the texts from Sirach and Proverbs about holy Wisdom shows the Mother of God in a triple role. She is the prototype of worship, ceaselessly glorifying God (the doxological role conferred by her Assumption, when she exults in the fullness of salvation as the embodied person she is [cf. 5.2.1]). She is the icon of the Church celebrating her liturgical play in the world, vis-à-vis the majesty of the Most High (in an innocence so complete it requires a wholly undistorted origin, an "Immaculate Conception," fitting for the Bride of God [cf. 5.6.2–5.6.3]). She is also the sign of the genuinely human quality of the contact between creatures and the Trinitarian outreach in Jesus Christ (this woman is the only created person who belongs to the hypostatic order of the Trinity itself [cf. 3.5]). I am struck by the parallelism between the God-bearer, *Dei Genetrix*, who brought forth the Word in the mystery of the nativity, and the Church, fruit of the Incarnation, who in her liturgical actions gives birth in the sacramental flesh and blood of the Eucharist to the real presence of the King.[31]

5.5.2   After the Mother of God, I hold in veneration the holy apostles who remain not only the foundation stones of the Church's origin (cf. Rev 21:14) but also the eschatological judges, equipped with the merciful judgment of the Lamb, who on their thrones await the Church's members at her end (cf. Matt 19:28).

5.5.3   Save St. John, the apostles are numbered among the martyrs, who themselves were the first to be recognized as privileged coinherers in the mysteries, thanks to the total nature of their conformation to the Son in the Sacrifice that climaxed his mission. I treasure especially, not least for its resonance with the title of this work, the prayer of St. Polycarp of Smyrna: "I beseech you, because you have deigned at this day and hour that, numbered among the martyrs, I may receive a part in the Chalice of Christ for the resurrection in the eternal life of body and soul, incorruptibly, through the Holy Spirit."[32] Since the army of martyrs includes not only celebrities but also the barely known and even the anonymous, the double list of saints in the Roman Canon appropriately singles out—after, in the first case, the Mother of God (and her spouse) together with the apostles, and in the second case the Precursor and Baptist, John—a careful selection of both these kinds of names. Before the eucharistic consecration, the *Communicantes* list aligns in hierarchical order six bishops (five of them popes), followed by two clerics, then four laymen, and most of these are obscure, while the second list, after the consecration at the *Nobis quoque*, names the protomartyr Stephen, followed by seven men (ranged in hierarchical order of office) and seven women, most of whose cases almost nothing is known. "These are properly the true representatives of the unknown heroes of the first Christian centuries who, because of their glorious death for Christ, continued to live on in the minds and hearts of men. But their death for Christ was likewise their triumph with Christ, and that is enough to have their names serve as symbols of that blessed lot which we beg God we, along with our own departed, might share at least to some extent."[33] Just as ancient Christians begged the prayers of living confessors, so the Church calls habitually on the intercession of the saints to assist the faithful; no prayer is restricted to the lone hypostasis thanks to the open flow of interhypostatic relations in the coinherence which we know by faith to be communion in Jesus Christ.

5.6   The Principle Underlying the Transposition of the Mysteries: The Work of Grace

The transposition of the mysteries of Christ into the sacramental mysteries of the Church is for the sake of the transformation of human existence itself into new life in Christ (cf.2.3.5; 2.4.7). Such transforming of existence through the transposition of the mysteries is, I maintain, the principal locus for understanding the distinction between the orders of nature and grace. Here above all, it is apparent that the supernatural is the sheer gift of God, which cannot be obtained by one's efforts, but only through gratuitous grace.

5.6.1 "The supernatural"—the provision by God of means duly proportioned to our more than natural end—implies that the form of natural life is insufficient for humanity in the present dispensation. That natural form is not enough to attain the end God holds out to man by filling up the chalice of the world with his own divine life (cf. 2.4.1; 2.4.6–2.4.7). "If we can say that man, since his creation, carries the possibility of hearing the call of God for the supernatural end for which he destined him, this does not mean that that possibility of hearing is already the call, and that the supernatural to which man is called is already present in him."[34] Grace is not a *sequela creationis*, entailed in the creation of humanity, and yet there *is* an aspect of continuity: man made in the image of God has a real capacity to receive the grace of God if it be given him (cf. 2.2–2.2.1).

5.6.2 Worse than insufficient, the natural form of humanity as found in the postlapsarian creation is, however, seriously awry. The first Fall is the loss of Eden itself, that is, human nature as it came from the hand of the triune Creator. In the words of St. Cyril, "Nature became ill from sin by the disobedience of one man, that is, from Adam. Thus was the multitude brought forth in sin; not that they shared in the error of Adam—they did not yet exist but because they shared his nature, fallen under the law of sin." And the Alexandrian doctor goes on to say that just as in Adam nature became ill from corruption, so in Christ it "recovered its health" by becoming liberatingly subject to the Father.[35] This malaise is a cosmic condition from which deliverance was needed. It is as persons who *appropriate fallen nature*—in principle, by coming into existence in it, and in act, by making it their own through personal ratification of moral disorder—that the members of the human species are a guilty race (cf. 2.3.4). While for the Reformers, pardon of sin is accorded solely by confidence in the divine promises and not by charity (which, in their eyes, belongs to sanctification, not justification), for the prince of the apostles, St. Peter, conversion, accorded by grace, is the condition of pardon (cf. Acts 3:19). Without turning from sin, which means simultaneously turning to the Lord, there is no sanation of the human condition (cf. 3.4.1).

5.6.3 In consequence of this twofold lack—the insufficiency of natural form and its corruption—man, called to know and love God as he is, enters the world with an "inconsolable wound.[36]

5.6.4 The principal work of grace is holiness. By counterdistinction to liberation theology, I take the order of God in the soul to be prerequisite for divine order in the social realm. "The natural loves are summoned to become modes of Charity while also remaining the natural loves they are"[37] (cf. 5.4.4). I trace the soteriological deficiencies of liberation theology to a minimalising of the scope of original righteousness, man's situation before the Fall. I agree with Mircea Eliade: desacralised man appears to have undergone a second Fall in which even the memory of Eden is lost to him.[38] The antidote for such amnesia is sanctifying grace, the new nature God bestows on the sinner in justification, healing the effects of original sin and orienting his powers to God in Christ by the Holy Spirit, thus bringing about the indwelling of the divine Trinity, to be enjoyed now by faith but to be revealed definitively in glory (cf. 2.3.4; 5.2.2–5.2.4; 6.4.3). There is—and here I part company from "nonprudent" romanticism (cf. 2.2.2)—no possible cure for nature nor return to the stable order of reason in its full amplitude save by integral recognition of the rights of the supernatural in acceptance of the evangelical vocation. The Utopian illusions (Marxian or Rousseauian) and Liberal aberrations of modern culture derive from a denial of the reality of original sin. Since sin is, for the children of Adam, acquiescence in false order (not origination thereof), grace, by subverting the established disorder, restores joy at once in creation and creation's Lord. As in St. Augustine's theology of the *delectatio victrix*, grace overwhelms free will (which, however, still retains its freedom of choice) by calling forth an unfailing, conquering delight in God. Such love for God as delectable fulfills the life of persons: on the one hand, it rejoices in God's endless beauty and goodness for God's own sake, while on the other, "love would no longer be love if it renounced its accompanying joy."[39] It is sacrificially theocentric and humanely eudaimonistic at the same time: our final end is, as we have said, God himself, but beatifically (cf. 5.4.1). With regard to predestination of particular persons to that end, we affirm the election of the blessed, without reference to their merits, but not the reprobation, without reference to their demerits, of the damned, for free choice can "nihilate" the approach of grace through that "surd" which is sinful aversion to God (cf. 2.3.6).

5.7   The Icons of Grace: Society and State, Household and Friendship, Arts and Sciences

The love of God indwelling us through sanctification is uncreated grace; its effects in us, insofar as they are the work of love, are created grace, for sanctifying grace alters a person's condition in relation to God. Engracement means a real, ontological, formal, yet analogical participation in the divine life (2.3.1), making us the Father's adopted sons, since adoptive sonship is a participated likeness of the eternal filiation of the Son of God (cf. the account of Baptism in 5.3.1). Hence the icons of grace must be Christocentric. From this there follows the social reign of Christ on the macrolevel of society and state and on the microlevel of household and friendship group.

5.7.1 I acknowledge the historic vocation of the Church to guide the polis. The Church's political identity derives from the Paschal Mystery, which itself culminates in the Exaltation of Christ as Lord. In a civil society that seeks to iconise the Church's communional life as an inaugural form of the Kingdom (cf. 2.4.7), person and sociality will each be accorded their proportionate importance, but beyond such formalities—the dialectic of subsidiarity and solidarity—her task is the proclamation of the reign of Christ the King. I agree with Henry Edward Manning: wherever possible, it is right that "the Church never withdraws from the State as such, which would be to abandon the natural society of man to its own maladies and mortality."[40] "Christendom," however, offers no mere medicine for social disintegration but a pattern of social holiness based on charity, whereas secularism, which is practical atheism, takes even the presuppositions of the natural virtues, such as duty, honour, and modesty, for eventual victims. As to the contradictory attempt to uphold ethical values deriving from Christian dogma while dispensing with the dogma itself, it can only bring frustration.

5.7.2 The social organism, transformed redemptively in the supernatural society of the Church, has its living cells in the family and in friends. By its fundamental order the family witnesses to the supernatural goal, joining its members in a scheme of differentiated responsibility and subordination that is modeled on the work of Christ vis-à-vis his Church-Bride, for whom he gave himself in love (cf. the account of Matrimony in 5.3.1). So likewise does the testimony of friends, when their mutual service includes the copresence of Christ; for two persons to become one without absorption by one of the other "they must become three."[41] Like everything human, in the messianic age of divine-human union (cf. 3.3), such natural microsocieties cannot now reach their ends except through transformation of a Christ-related kind. My statements on these topics are schematic. Yet their brief figuring in systematics furnishes a right orientation for movement toward the final *telos* of nuptiality and friendship within the totality of thinking about revelation and the sensibility it inspires.

5.7.3 The arts and sciences cannot be separated from theology since human nature in its creative and cognitive enterprises cannot be severed from grace. I consider all aspects of culture potential bearers of theological meaning. I admire the audacity of Dorothy Sayers, for whom the Church "must insist strongly that the whole material universe is an expression and incarnation of the creative energy of God, as a book or a picture is the material expression of the creative soul of the artist. For that reason, all good and creative handling of the material universe is holy and beautiful, and all abuse of the material universe is a crucifixion of the body of Christ. [Thus] . . . the exploitation of man or of matter for commercial uses stands condemned, together with all debasement of the arts and perversions of the intellect."[42] While such respect for creation is indeed a presupposition of the grace-life, the arts and sciences are, I submit, capable of a further, genuinely iconic, role in forwarding the message of revelation and its salvific fruit. This occurs when, so far as *the arts* are concerned, the practice of the arts takes as its content a sacral poetics for which the incarnate Word is the central reference point of artistic sensibility. Correspondingly, for *the sciences,* it transpires when the scientific disciplines are housed within a sacral cosmology for which the hominisation of the Logos is the nodal point, unifying in a single nexus—as Incarnation does—both the natural and the human sciences. Elsewhere, I have proposed Gerard Manley Hopkins and Paul Claudel as examples of such a "sacral poetics."[43] And as to a "sacral cosmology" capable of integrating the findings of the natural sciences, I regard the attempt of Pierre Teilhard de Chardin, though flawed, as indicating the general direction of desirable advance.[44] I note that Sayers's alignment of the material world with the body of Christ (actually, she speaks of identification, but I allow for the demands of a literary trope) depends for its validity on the claim that the Logos, by becoming incarnate, entered into a solidarity with the cosmos as a whole, which carries implications for the entire created pattern (cf. Newman's reflections on the relation of Christ to the universe in 3.5).

5.7.4 I wish contemporary multiculturalism to be comprehended within the framework of a shared human culture generously conceived; since our species is ordered to the same supernatural goal, it militates against its nature if its culture is too radically diverse. The unity of the *humanum*—which is far from excluding a variety rooted in the particularities of memory (cf. 4.2.4)—is necessarily presupposed in the proclamation of a single Gospel of salvation for all the world.

5.8   *The Extension of the Pattern: Mission and Dialogue*

The extension of the Christ pattern, as the greater mysteries are transposed into the lesser, is the normative way of salvation. But the pattern cannot be apprehended without the elevation of human knowing in the act of Christian faith (cf. 2.2.6). Hence I affirm the priority of mission over dialogue, though I value dialogue as a sharing of speech that, whenever truth-bearing, carries reference to the Logos (cf. introduction).

5.8.1 While mission is universal in its scope (cf. Matt 28:18-20), Christians have in its regard a special obligation to Israel, a debt of gratitude for the grafting of the wild olive branch onto the parent stock (Rom 11:17). I am a qualified supersessionist. I accept that the covenants continue to hold for Israel insofar as they are promises, but they do not constitute a parallel to the new and everlasting covenant in Jesus Christ. Israel has recognized the triune God in his common nature, the unoriginated I AM, but not in the intradivine relations whereby the Father is the unoriginated Origin of the Word and Spirit, and without this recognition the messianic fulfillment of her vocation in Jeshua (Jesus) cannot be grasped (cf. 6.1.4–6.1.5). I make my own the words of Augustine in *In Answer to the Jews*: "Dearly beloved, whether the Jews receive these divine testimonies with joy or with indignation, nevertheless, when we can, let us proclaim them with great love for the Jews. Let us not proudly glory against the broken branches, let us rather reflect by whose grace it is, and by how much mercy, and on what root, we have been grafted. Then, not savouring of pride, but with a deep sense of humility, not insulting with presumption but rejoicing with trembling, let us say, 'Come yet and let us walk in the light of the Lord.' "[45] That "light" is, in this perspective, the eschatological Light that never sets, for I heed the teaching of St. Paul that the entry of Jewry into the Church (in more than occasional representative persons) is a sign of the consummation of world history, as the original people of the Promise come into what is their own (Rom 11:25-27).

5.9   Total Interpretation: Universal History

I concur with C. S. Lewis that while "all history in the last resort must be held by Christians to be a story with a divine plot . . . [i]t is, as known to men, only an overall plot."[46] With Chesterton and David Jones, I affirm a "hermeneutic centred on Christ and His Crucifixion, the pivotal person and event in history. . . . This belief provides a focal point to which [these writers] relate all other persons, events, rites, and myths" (cf. introduction; 3.1.1).[47] With Christopher Dawson, I hold that "every Christian has his 'philosophy of history' given in his religion; he cannot make a new one for himself."[48] Christ inaugurates the last age of history; the progression to the End has commenced (cf. 3.2.1–3.2.2; 3.4.6–3.4.8; 4.3.2). "The last hour is long but it *is* the last hour."[49]

Source: M. V. Alpatov, *Early Russian Icon Painting* (Moscow: Iskusstvo, 1984), plate 196.

Chapter 6

The Holy Trinity as Matrix and Goal of Persons and the World

Nikifor Savin, The New Testament Trinity

This icon shows the Son enthroned on the Father's lap with the Holy Spirit as their living Go-Between. The Trinity, attended by the adoring angels, is revealed in the Gospel, and the symbols of the four evangelists appear in the points of the star. Only by means of that Gospel do we know the Alpha, the Source from which creation came, and the Omega, the goal to which we tend.

6.1   The Trinity as Expositionally Taught

The phrase "expositionally taught" might seem a pleonasm, but I shall introduce a distinction between teaching expounded and teaching enacted (cf. 6.2). Meanwhile, I receive the thesis of St. Thomas for which all the articles of faith are precontained in the two primary *credibilia*, as found in the letter to the Hebrews (Heb 11:6). Just as the assertion that God is "anxious for the salvation of all men" is included within "all that God designs in time so as to bring men to . . . beatitude," so the assertion that "God is" comprises by its reference to divine being "all that we believe to exist eternally in God, in which our beatitude consists," that is, the mystery of the Trinity.[1] Accepting as I do the reading of the New Testament found by reference to the canon in its entirety against the backcloth of Tradition as a whole and, within that acceptance, maintaining, moreover, the substantial historicity of the Gospel according to St. John, I find the mystery of Father, Son, and Spirit, in their unitive interrelation, to be the teaching of Scripture, issuing from the prophetically inspired mind assumed by the Logos in Incarnation: Jesus Christ (cf. 1.1.1; 3.1–3.1.2; 3.2–3.2.1; 3.5).

6.1.1 Though the confession of the one God is crucial for the monotheism of Israel and the synthesis of reason and faith on which systematics builds, the unity of God must never be thought without his threefoldness. I find no difference between the Greek and Latin traditions in this regard.[2] In the East, St. Gregory the Theologian declares, "No sooner do I conceive of the One than I am enlightened by the radiance of the Three; no sooner do I distinguish them than I am carried back to the One. . . . When I contemplate the Three together I see but one

Luminary, and cannot divide or measure out the undivided light."[3] And for the West, the Creed called *Quicumque* confesses, "We worship one God in Trinity and the Trinity in unity; without confusing the Persons, without dividing the substance; other is indeed the Person of the Father, other that of the Son, other that of the Holy Spirit. But the Father, the Son, and the Holy Spirit have one same divinity, an equal glory, a same eternal majesty."[4]

6.1.2 I hold God to be plenary being for which the essence of God is energetic and his energies essential. I thus accept the Palamite distinction,[5] but only in order to overcome it by reference to the affirmation that God is supremely the Living One. "But the Lord is the true God; he is the living God and the everlasting King" (Jer 10:10). I recall how for Aristotle the being of living things is their life, understood as an immanent operation.[6] Their being is *energeia*, the substantive operation in which their active existence consists. The more operative a being is, the more perfect it is, and this is uniquely true of the Fount of being in his triune life, as well as at a secondary level, in his creating, sustaining, and consummating the world. "My Father is working still, and I am working" (John 5:17),[7] for "as the Father has life in himself so he has granted to the Son also to have life in himself" (John 5:26). Within this energetic being of his, the freedom of God is eternally constituted as a mutual self-emptying and self-offering grounded in the plenitude of divine life (cf. 6.2.2; 6.2.5). Its Source is the Father who gives all he has in begetting the Son and bringing forth the Spirit, thus constituting Son and Spirit as equals who through the medium of the common essence actualise their relatedness and freely offer themselves to each other in a communion of loving life (cf. 3.5; 3.5.2). I decline to follow that exaggerated personalism which would leave the divine nature without content, save as the communion of the Three.

6.1.3 It follows that God is Love (cf. 1 John 4:8)—but I reject the claim that an "agapeology" can replace ontology in an account of the mystery of God. I agree with Etienne Gilson: "To say that God is love is not to say that He is not being; on the contrary, it is to affirm it a second time for God's love is but the sovereign liberality of Being, who, in super-abundant plenitude, loves Himself both in Himself and in all his possible participations,"[8] since, while generating love in himself in the Word and the Spirit, he causes it in others as finite participations of his life. The Christian identification of the love of God as central and organizing in any revelationally attuned account of the divine attributes does not, however, license neglect of the dimensions of divine being thus theologically centred and organized. I commend the presentation of the perfections of divine being in the school of St. Thomas, unsurpassed in this respect in its integration of Scripture with metaphysics.[9]

6.1.4 Initially, the names of God, like his Law, were given to the people of Israel, the covenant with whom, in an otherwise pervasive situation of post-Fall idolatry, was the primal means of God's restoring humankind to friendship with himself.[10] Prepared in the disclosures of the Old Testament about the "Word of the Lord" and God's "Spirit," the mystery of the Trinity enters into human discourse as declared by Jesus Christ on the basis of his fullness of salvific knowledge, which pertains to him as the prophetic mind hypostatically united to the Father's subsistent Word. While the Pentateuch knows God as Father of Israel (Deut 32:6), the Former

Prophets and Psalms know God as Father of the messianic King (2 Sam 7:14; Ps 2; 89), and the Wisdom books speak of a special paternity of God in regard to the just (Sir 22:27–23:6), in his own teaching Jesus declares God to be not only Father of his hearers but to have "Father" (*Abba*) as his own personal name. It is only through the Only-Begotten that we know the first Trinitarian Person to be Father entirely, wholly, and uniquely. The same situation pertains in the case of the Breath, the Holy Spirit. While for the Sapiential writers it is by the breath of God's mouth that the heavens were made and for the Former and Later Prophets the Spirit of the Lord comes upon judges and prophets, it is only with the promises of Jesus in the High Priestly Prayer (John 14–16) and the visible gift of the Spirit at Pentecost (Acts 2:1-4) that the disciples adequately grasped the distinct personality of the Spirit that was to be given them. In the insufflation of the Johannine Pentecost (John 20:22), when the Risen One gives the Spirit to the Church by breathing on the apostles, we see with St. Bernard the "kiss" of the Spirit's being, now disclosed not only for our utilization but for our contemplation too. "The kiss is not the corporeal breath [of Christ], but the indivisible Spirit given in this breath so that we might understand that he proceeds equally from the Lord and from the Father as a kiss common to the one who embraces and the one who is embraced. . . . The Father embraces, the Son is embraced, the Spirit is the Kiss as imperturbable peace and indivisible unity of the Father and the Son."[11] The love-mysticism of the Church, which is the essence of the spirituality of the saints (cf. 1.1.2), depends on a sharing in this "kiss."

6.1.5 Belief in the Holy Trinity is, therefore, salvationally crucial; as St. Thomas declares in the *Summa theologiae*, the Trinity was revealed "principally to give us a right understanding of the salvation of the human race, which is effected by the incarnate Son and the gift of the Holy Spirit,"[12] and, more briefly, in its predecessor the *Writing on the Sentences*, "The knowledge of the Trinity in unity is the fruit and goal of our whole life."[13] Or as a modern Thomist has written, "The three Persons are the principal co-operating agents in our rebirth to life in that godhead which they are; a rebirth entailing the conscious recognition of them which is our faith. The Christian God *is* the three Persons; hence whoever does not know them, in some degree, is simply not a Christian."[14] The adoptive filiation we receive from God is ascribed ("appropriated") to the Father as its *author*, since the Father acts as author or source of the Son and the Spirit by whom he joins us to himself: to the Son as its *model*, for the Son acts as Son of the Father, giving us a share in his filiation; and to the Holy Spirit as he who *imprints filiation on us*, for the Spirit acts as Spirit of the Son, communicating to us existence as sons and daughters of the Father. Our goal as persons is loving union with the supreme Beauty in his triune exchange of life and love (cf. 2.3.2; 6.4.3).

6.1.6   Though the Father is in the Godhead the Principle-without-a-principle, the Origin of Son and Spirit, with St. Athanasius I hold the Son and Spirit to be divine not in virtue of hierarchical ordering to the Father but by a numerical identity of essence and thus to be equally God. With the Cappadocian Fathers, I also acclaim the Godhead as "undivided in Three who are distinct,"[15] with each hypostasis inhering relationally in the other two. I admit here two equally important and irreducible perspectives. I indicate their complementarity by adding with St.

Thomas that the relative properties of the persons (father-hood in the case of the Father, sonship in the case of the Word, procession in the case of the Spirit) are really identi-cal with the divine essence. The persons are, therefore, "subsistent relations" whose being and activity coincide with the total reality of God.[16] In this way, the teaching of the angelic doctor serves to unify the tradition of the Greek fathers, as well as to manifest its unity of outlook with that of the Latins (cf. 6.1.1).

6.1.7 In regard to the origination of the persons, I find useful the following comment: "The processions of the Son and the Holy Spirit are necessary in God, but we can-not understand why—for the Father has no 'need' of the Son (in the human sense of the word). It is a necessity of splendour, an unforeseeable superabundance of perfection itself—it is an eternal luxury ('luxury' comes from *lux* which means light)."[17] I respect as philosophically helpful the Augustinian-Thomist understanding of the proces-sions of the Word and the Spirit in terms of the immanent operations of knowledge and love (in the transcendent freedom of God as pure spirit, divine being prolongs itself into self-knowing and self-loving in a way that is fecund of personal—indeed, interpersonal—life), though I regard the account of Richard of St. Victor as the more theologi-cally compelling (cf. 6.2). Stressing love as the central identifying trait of the divine nature—"God is love" (1 John 4:8; cf. 6.1.3)—Richard finds that love requires a tending to the other—which in God can only be the infinitely loveable, that is, Another within God; but then the Lover seeks a Third to share the regard in which he beholds the Beloved, so that he may be regarded by the Beloved as the Beloved is regarded by him. The divine society terminates, then, in Three, while opening the way to further images of itself in creation through Word and Spirit.[18] I note, however, that for the Thomas of the *Writing on the Sentences*, the generation of the Son in the mode of understanding already entails (prior to reference to the Spirit) the love that enters into every divine act and in a sovereign fashion into the immanent processions.[19] Thus I hold there to be no necessary contradiction between the Thomasian and Ricardian accounts.[20]

6.1.8 In the relationality of the Trinitarian Persons, I find the root of the significance of persons-in-their-relations in the cosmic process, for created persons bear the "trace" of the Trinity (2.3.6; 2.4.6–2.4.7). The energies of the Trinity can be expressed beyond the inner-Trinitarian communion in the divine essence, freely manifesting themselves in God's relation with his creation where Father, Son, and Spirit seek to realize a nexus of interrelatedness with other beings. As found in their relation with the world, the divine energies are an invitation to creatures to enter by grace into that communion event of the triune life. This is realized through the Incarnation and Paschal Mystery whereby in the Mystical Body of Christ human persons are united with him in just such a nexus of interrelatedness, as human nature is healed and becomes the medium of communion, a cause of unity, not division (cf. 4.2.1–4.2.2; 5.2.3)—albeit in fullness only at the End. As Persons who are subsistent relations, the Trinity must be the presupposition of this process. While relationships in what is not the Trinity can never actually be *identical with substance* (which is the case in God), the more beings enter into engraced relations which codefine them, the more they approach asymptotically the triune

Archetype where each Person is an "I" only in relation to the other Two; in their communion the Three (compare the intimacy of Jesus' relation with Father and Spirit) are reciprocally conscious with a consciousness diversely possessed by each. I note that relationality is not opposed to personal identity. Human persons, like the divine Persons, are "incommunicable": they have a noninterchangeable, irreducible identity—but precisely without this identity no genuine spiritual communication (and thus interrelation) is thinkable.

6.2 The Trinity as Found in the Paschal Mystery

As "expositionally taught," the revelation of the Trinity turns crucially on the doctrine of Jesus himself—for which I accept as witness the historical value of the Fourth Gospel (cf. 6.1.1) as the work of an eyewitness of that Word "in whom are hid all the riches of wisdom and knowledge" (Col 2:3).[21] But the teaching is marvelously confirmed by the Paschal Mystery, where it is not expounded but *enacted*. I accept with St. Thomas that Christ "carried his cross as a teacher his candelabrum, as a support for the light of his teaching, because for believers the message of the cross is the power of God."[22] By coming in Christ in his own person to a lost world, the eternal God made known in painful yet efficacious act, and not only in teaching, both himself and his love for the fallen creation. The triune relationality occurs in the history of Jesus, without its being in any way the case that the economy retroactively reshapes the self-relatedness of the divine Persons. I reject interpretation of Trinitarian narration read sequentially, as though the flow of narration corresponded to a temporally developing relationality within the triune God. It is enough to say of the Christ of Good Friday and Easter, with Mother Julian of Norwich, "Where Jesus appears, the Blessed Trinity is understood."[23]

6.2.1 I ask, however, How should we understand the ontology of the act of the divine being, in the light of which the narrative can be rendered coherently as an account of the character of the divine life? In the light of the narrative of the divine self-involvement that climaxes in the Paschal Mystery, there is egregious confirmation of what I have inferred from the "expositionally taught": divine being is through and through the being of love (cf. 6.1.2–6.1.3). In the exercise of the divine nature by the Three, we are further instructed on that love's hypostatically character-istic mode (cf. 6.2.2).

6.2.2 Specifically, the love shown in the Paschal Mystery is kenotic—self-emptying—or sacrificial love (cf. 3.5.2).[24] With Sergei Bulgakov and Balthasar, though deploring their rhetorical excesses, I affirm that the Paschal Mystery reveals by analogy the eternal, mutual kenosis of Father and Son in the ecstasy of love that is the Holy Spirit—for Father and Spirit differ from the Son only in their "relations of opposi-tion" (respectively, fatherhood and procession, rather than generation) and in naught else. Each such relation involves a sacrifice, a "kenosis," an act of self-humiliation.

6.2.3 Thus, as to the Father: From all eternity the Father possesses his divine nature only as giving it to the Son. Such fatherhood, writes Bulgakov, is the very image of love, since "he who loves wants to possess himself not in himself but outside himself, so as to give his 'I' to this other 'I' in such a way that he is identified with him; [he wants] to manifest his 'I' by a spiritual birth, in the Son who is the living image of the Father."[25] So the Father's begetting of the Son is the primal act of possessing the divine nature where the Father has his nature by passing it on, through giving it away.

6.2.4 As to the Son: Just as the Father wants to possess himself only in the Son, so the Son does not want to possess the divine nature for himself. He wants rather to offer his personal selfhood, his *seitas*, in sacrifice to the Father (cf. 3.5.2). He is the Word, yes. But that means he is the *Father's* Word, not his own. When the Holy Spirit proceeds from the Father through the Son (or, as the Middle Byzantine theologians would say, by "resting on" the Son), a triumphant testimony is given to the sacrificial exchange which joins Father and Son forevermore. For this sacrificial exchange is what produces the Holy Spirit.

6.2.5 As to the Spirit: In the Trinity the Spirit exists by showing the Son to the Father and the Father to the Son. He is the moment of their mutual love. The Holy Spirit possesses the divine nature as the joy of sacrificial love. He is God as the beatitude of the love of Father and Son, its perfect fruit. Thus for Balthasar, since each of the hypostases is identical with the divine essence, the whole divine nature is congruent with self-gift (cf. 6.2.1). Though the essence is indivisibly one, whilst the Persons are three in number, the former must be such as to account for fitting possession by the latter (a key assertion of Bulgakov's sophiology too). This would justify theologically, in its Source and in a Trinitarian manner, the claim that self-giving love is the primordial, transcendental characteristic of being, which Balthasar's friend Gustav Siewerth asserted when speaking philosophically of the world, of what is involved in bestowal on recipients of the *actus essendi* (cf. 2.2.3).[26]

6.2.6 In the light of Pentecost, we can say of the Holy Spirit that it is he who enables the world to be in Christ and Christ to be in the world. For this reason he is the Spirit of the Church, since the "renovated creation" in Christ is an "ecclesialised cosmos" (cf. 3.4.8). The communion of the faithful in the Church flows from the Trinitarian communion; what St. Cyprian had seen of the Trinitarian matrix of the Church, St. Augustine expresses in terms of the Spirit as the consubstantial Charity of the Father and the Son.[27] "The society of the unity of the Church of God, outside of which there is no remission of sins, is as it were the proper work of the Holy Spirit, with whom the Father and the Son cooperate, because the Holy Spirit is in some manner their fellowship."[28] With this I compare the words of the American Dominican Romanus Cessario: "He who in the depths of the divine reality is the perfect image expressed by the Father and who together with the Father breathes forth personal love as the bond of fellowship, replicates this divine communion within the medium of his humanity and his human history for our sakes."[29]

6.3   *The Indwelling Trinity*

With St. Augustine I confess that the person living with the theological virtues can find in his or her soul a refraction of God's love for it: the "presence of God as the enabling and animating principle of the soul's own loving of God."[30] Here the trio of lover (the self), Beloved (God), and the love that binds them together function anagogically, in a manner cognate with the eschatological reading of Scripture itself (cf. 3.2.2), enabling the faithful to experience their love as *Donum*, the divine Gift—that is, the Holy Spirit who eternally binds the Son to the Father in love and now in time carries human persons through the Son to loving union with the Source whence the Son comes forth. "Our Christian loving experienced as a unitive force is a faint reflection of the unity of Father and Son in their Spirit."[31]

6.3.1 Trinitarian presence to the self is not only, however, experiential (and fortunately so, for its entry into consciousness may turn on the contingencies of natural and supernatural gifts: particular temperaments, particular charisms). That presence is also ontological and, here, charity is its sign.

> The soul is made like to God by grace. Hence for a divine person to be sent to anyone by grace, there must be a likening of the soul to the divine person Who is sent, by some gift of grace. Because the Holy Ghost is Love, the soul is assimilated to the Holy Ghost by the gift of charity; hence the mission of the Holy Ghost is according to the mode of charity. Whereas the Son is the Word, not any sort of word, but one Who breathes forth Love. Hence Augustine says, "The Word we speak of is knowledge with love." Thus the Son is sent not in accordance with every and any kind of intellectual perfection, but according to the intellectual illumination, which breaks forth into the affection of love.[32]

The divinization of persons is impossible without the transformative indwelling of the Trinity, bringing those primordially made in his image (cf. 3.5–3.5.1) to their definitive or eschatological form (cf. 2.3.5).

6.4   The Trinity as Protology and Eschatology

I consider that in the light of the expounded Trinity, the Trinity of the Paschal Mystery, and the indwelling Trinity, which together make up the *theologia viatorum*, it is also possible, then, to speak of the Trinity of the Beginning and the Trinity of the End.

6.4.1   Though the Trinity is revealed in history it is primordially active in creation itself: it is the sole principle of the universe. The generation of the Word and the procession of the Spirit are the exemplary cause of creation; the loving Wisdom of the Son and the liberal Goodness of the Holy Spirit are the raison d'être of the entire production of creatures. Creation flows from a Trinitarian matrix, and wherever ontological triads are discerned we can speak of vestiges of a Trinitarian ontology given with the absolute beginnings of the world. "The care of God over all things matches the mode of their being. Now it is connatural to a human being . . . to be guided by the seen towards the unseen; this is why the invisible things of God had to be made known through the visible. With his creatures as evidence God has in some way pointed to himself and the eternal processions of the persons."[33]

6.4.2   Congruently, I do not reject the possibility of proto-Trinitarian motifs in the mythopoiesis of the religious cultures of the pagans. With C. S. Lewis, I hold that myths may be blurred dreams and intimations of the events which are at the core of cosmic history, a "real though unfocussed gleam of the divine truth falling on human imagination."[34] They can awaken in the reader a longing for something beyond his grasp, an echo of the paradisal apprehension of Adam in the Beginning, an apprehension which was itself a first adumbration of the vision of God at the End (cf. 5.6.4).

6.4.3 The relations of the divine Persons with human persons have as their purpose to manifest the divine Persons to the human persons so that the human may participate in the divine (cf. 2.3.1). In the fully realized Kingdom, contemplation will consist in enraptured gaze upon the Trinity in the universal fellowship of the saints in the consummated world, anticipated now in the single-minded dedication to the Lord of the Church's monastics, whether women or men.[35] We shall be the perfect image of the Trinity when, in a triune activity of our own, our memory and intelligence and will possess—through modeling on the mind and heart of the incarnate Word—the Father, the Son, and the Holy Spirit in recognition, knowledge, and love (cf. 2.3.6). "Just as it has been said that the procession of the persons [from the Father] is the reason for the production of creatures by their first principle, so is it also the reason of their return toward their end: for just as it is by the Son and the Holy Spirit that we are created, so it is by them that we are reunited to the ultimate end."[36] The divine processions are not only the efficient and exemplary causes of creation; they are thus its final causes too. In the words of Balthasar, "The Father produced the creation in the Son and for the glory of the Son; but the Son created and saved it for the glory of the Father in order to offer it, once made perfect, to the Father (cf. 1 Cor 15:24-28); finally, the Spirit illumines it not in order to reveal himself but to reveal the infinite love between the Father and the Son and to incorporate this love in creation."[37] I agree with Balthasar (again) in the final volume of his theological dramatics: divine being, and thus fontal being, in which all other being participates, is ultimately the generosity of love. Being lost in wonder at the being and action of the Trinity brings to its culmination the admiration of rational creatures at the beauty of the world (cf. 2.3.2).

6.4.4 The perfect acceptance of God's extravagant libation is heaven, and the learning so to do, in the hope-filled pain that heals and expiates our declensions from love, is purgatory, the antechamber of heaven's court. How then shall we think of the rank antitheses of love? They are the bitter fruit of nihilism, whether tacit or explicit. They are, in spirit or in thought, entry on the way of *privatio entis*, the individual choosing the real impossibility that is countercreation (cf. 6.2.5). Hell is the latter's name.

6.4.5 Nihilism and its contrary, the affirmation of being as generosity, are the supreme existential alternatives of human life, furnishing in this regard the antiform and form of human possibility (cf. 2.2). They are, respectively, existence without and against grace and existence with and under grace (cf. 5.6.1–5.6.2), that grace which is always the grace of Christ, the Trinitarian Son made man (cf. 3.4.1).

6.4.6 It is in letting the soul, the microcosm, and the world, the macrocosm, be the receptacle for all the generosity the Trinity pours forth that the Chalice of God fills to the brim (cf. 1.4.1, 3.4.2).

Source: M. V. Alpatov, *Early Russian Icon Painting* (Moscow: Iskusstvo, 1984), plate 163.

Laus Deo et Maria!

Concluding Icon

Icon of ca. 1500, The Mother of God in Whom All Creation Rejoices
Dormition Cathedral, Moscow

The icon pictures the assembly of creation around the Mother of God, who in her person gathers up creation's praise to the Trinity, which is thanksgiving for the consummation of God's creative and redemptive work. The varied ranks of the faithful represent humankind in its diversity. The flora stand for the natural world. The outlines of a temple which surmount the whole indicate how this is an ecclesialised cosmos, where nature has been taken up into that glorifying of God which lies at the heart of all the activity of the Church.

Notes

Chapter 1

1. O. Brooke, "Towards a Theology of Connatural Knowledge," in idem., *Studies in Monastic Theology* (Kalamazoo, MI: 1980), pp. 232–49.

2. Thomas Aquinas, *Summa theologiae* IIa. IIae., q. 45, a. 2, citing 1 Cor 6:17. Unless otherwise noted, all translations into English are provided by the author. See more widely, A. Léonard, "L'Expérience spirituelle," in *Dictionnaire de spiritualité*, IV, 2 (Paris: 1960), pp. 2004–66; M. Dupuy, "Expérience spirituelle et théologie comme science," *Nouvelle Revue théologique* (1964), pp. 1137–62.

3. H. U. von Balthasar, "Theology and Holiness," in idem., *Explorations in Theology I: The Word Made Flesh* (San Francisco: 1989), pp. 181–209.

4. Athanasius, *De synodis* 39.

5. J. Daniélou, S. J., *God and Us* (London: 1957), p. 182.

6. In 1914 Benedict XV's Congregation of Studies approved "Twenty-four Theses" as compatible with the philosophy of Thomas but said nothing about their compelling obedience; in renewing Leo XIII's appeal to Thomas as outstanding master, Pius XI in his 1923 encyclical *Studiorum ducem* declared, "Let none demand more from others than our mistress and mother the Church asks from all" (30).

7. F. A. von Staudenmaier, *Die christliche Dogmatik*, I (Freiburg: 1844), p. 13.

8. L. T. Zagzebski, "Vocatio philosophiae," in K. J. Clark, ed., *Philosophers Who Believe* (Downers Grove, IL: 1993), p. 240.

9. F. A. von Staudenmaier, *Encyklopädie der theologischen Wissenschaften als System der gesammten Theologie* (Mainz: 1840, 2nd edition), p. 22.

10. Ibid., p. 23.

Chapter 2

1. S. T. Coleridge, *The Friend*, ed. B. E. Rooke (London: 1969), I, p. 514.

2. I note the confidence expressed in the fundamental conceptual repertoire by John Paul II, *Fides et ratio* 96: the human intellect can fashion "certain basic concepts [that] retain their universal epistemological value and thus retain the truth of the propositions in which they are expressed."

3. J. J. Kockelmans, *The Metaphysics of Aquinas* (Leuven: 2001), p. 87. The prologue to St. Thomas's *Commentary on the Gospel according to John* has an especially concise summary: "Since all things which exist participate in existence [*esse*] and are beings by participation, there must necessarily be at the summit of all things something which is existence [*esse*] by its essence, i.e., whose essence is its existence. And this is God, who is the most sufficient, the most eminent, and the most perfect cause of the whole of existence, from whom all things that are participate existence [*esse*]," Thomas Aquinas, *Commentary on the Gospel of John, Chapters 1–5* (Washington, DC: 2010), prologue, no. 5, p. 2.

4. A major theme of H. U. von Balthasar, *Theo-Logic I: Truth of the World* (San Francisco: 2000).

5. W. Norris Clarke, "Person, Being, and St. Thomas," *Communio* XIX (1992), p. 607.

6. Examples are *eikôn*, "image"; *methexis*, "participation"; *homoiôsis*, "assimilation"; *paraplêsia*, "resemblance."

7. Compare Thomas Aquinas, *Summa theologiae* Ia., q. 79, a. 4.

8. H. E. Manning, *The Four Great Evils of the Day*, 8th edition (London: n.d.), p. 4, cited in J. Pereiro, *Cardinal Manning: An Intellectual Biography* (Oxford: 1998), p. 153.

9. W. Norris Clarke, S. J., *The One and the Many: A Contemporary Thomistic Metaphysics* (Notre Dame, IN: 2001).

10. R. A. te Velde, *Participation and Substantiality in Thomas Aquinas* (Leiden: 1995).

11. Dionysius, *The Mystical Theology* 2.

12. Plato, *Phaedrus* 249b–c.

13. M. J. Rees, *Just Six Numbers: The Deep Forces That Shape the Universe* (New York: 2000), p. 131.

14. J. S. von Drey, *Brief Introduction to the Study of Theology* (Notre Dame, IN: 1994), p. 44.

15. Thomas Aquinas, *Summa contra Gentiles* IV, 11; *Summa theologiae* Ia., q. 29, a. 3.

16. J. Coulson, *Newman and the Common Tradition: A Study in the Language of Church and Society* (Oxford: 1970), pp. 3–13.

17. "While the allegorical points to a reality we can also refer to directly, the symbol allows what is expressed in it to enter our world." C. Taylor, *Sources of the Self* (Cambridge: 1989), p. 379.

18. John Paul II, *Fides et ratio* 67.

19. Ibid., 12; compare the title of Balthasar's *Das Ganze im Fragment* (Einsiedeln: 1963).

20. T. T. Tollefsen, *The Christocentric Cosmology of St Maximus the Confessor* (Oxford: 2008), p. 55.

21. K. Anatolios, "Heaven and Earth in Byzantine Liturgy," *Antiphon* 5:3 (2000), p. 23.

22. Ibid.

23. John Paul II, *Fides et ratio* 12.

24. Ibid., 66.

25. A. Nichols, O. P., *From Hermes to Benedict XVI: Faith and Reason in Modern Catholic Thought* (Leominster: 2009), pp. 237–39.

26. R. Murray, S. J., *The Cosmic Covenant: Biblical Themes of Justice, Peace and the Integrity of Creation* (London: 1992).

27. Gregory Nazianzen, *Oration* 27, 3.

Chapter 3

1. M. Hengel, *The Four Gospels and the One Gospel of Jesus Christ* (London: 2000), p. 143: the "particular link of the Jesus tradition with particular tradents . . . is historically undeniable." Or, according to R. Bauckham, *Jesus and the Eyewitnesses: The Gospels as Eyewitness Testimony* (Grand Rapids, MI: 2006), p. 7, "if [it is] not 'historically undeniable,' then [it is] at least historically very probable."

2. P. Jenkins, *Hidden Gospels: How the Search for Jesus Lost Its Way* (New York: 2001).

3. Eusebius, *Historia ecclesiastica* II, 15, 1–2.

4. A concise modern defence of that order is offered in B. Orchard, O. S. B., *The Origin and Evolution of the Gospels* (London: 1993, 2nd edition).

5. Origen, *De principiis* IV, 2, 2.

6. I discovered this writer through the New York journal *First Things*, but for the theological hermeneutics he advocates (a recovery, indeed, of the ancient hermeneutic of the Church) at book length, see this coauthored work: J. J. O'Keefe and R. R. Reno, *Sanctified Vision: An Introduction to Early Christian Interpretation of the Bible* (Baltimore and London: 2005).

7. Augustine, *De doctrina christiana* I, 11.

8. J. Ratzinger, "Importance of the Fathers for the Structure of Faith," in idem., *Principles of Catholic Theology: Building Stones for a Fundamental Theology* (San Francisco: Ignatius Press, 1987), pp. 133–52.

9. B. F. Meyer, *Christus Faber: The Master Builder and the House of God* (Allison Park, PA: 1992), p. 71.

10. D. L. Dungan, "The Synoptic Problem: How Did We Get Our Gospels?" in W. Farmer, ed., *The International Bible Com-*

mentary: A Catholic and Ecumenical Commentary for the Twenty-First Century (Collegeville, MN: Liturgical Press, 1998), p. 1236.

11. W. Farmer, *The Gospel of Jesus: The Pastoral Relevance of the Synoptic Problem* (Louisville, KY: 1994).

12. H. de Lubac, S. J., *Scripture in the Tradition* (New York: [1968] 2000).

13. B. F. Meyer, *Christus Faber*, p. 12.

14. Troparion of the Annunciation in the Church of the Byzantine Rite.

15. J. Raymond, *Milton's Angels: The Early-Modern Imagination* (Oxford: 2010), p. 7.

16. The liturgical office of the Messiah is implied in his modeling on David. For the books of Chronicles the phrase the "mercies of David" (1 Chr 6:42) refers to his achievements on behalf of the true worship of God, and the Chronicler (a Levite, i.e., a male member of the house of Levi who was not, however, a descendant of Aaron) views the subsequent kings of Judah through the same lens—notably in connexion with the liturgy celebrated in the Temple.

17. H. U. von Balthasar, *The Glory of the Lord: A Theological Aesthetics*, vol. 7, *Theology: The New Covenant* (Edinburgh: 1989), p. 324.

18. E. L. Mascall, *Corpus Christi: Essays on the Church and the Eucharist* (London: 1965, 2nd edition), p. 102.

19. M. Barker, *Temple Theology: An Introduction* (London: 2004), p. 64.

20. D. B. Hart, "A Gift Exceeding Every Debt: An Eastern Orthodox Appreciation of Anselm's *Cur Deus homo*," *Pro Ecclesia* VII, 3 (1998), p. 347.

21. *Se dat suis manibus*. Thomas Aquinas, *Pange lingua*, strophe 4.

22. Dante, *Paradiso*, canto VII, 115–17. Translation by J. D. Sinclair (London: [1946] 1971), p.109.

23. Kontakion of the Transfiguration in the Church of the Byzantine Rite.

24. H. U. von Balthasar, *Love Alone: The Way of Revelation* (London: 1968), pp. 8, 112.

25. J. Daniélou, S. J., *Christ and Us* (London: 1961), p. 144.

26. Ibid.

27. At the Blessing of the Paschal Candle, on Holy Saturday, in the Church of the Roman Rite.

28. Kontakion of the Ascension in the Church of the Byzantine Rite.

29. H. U. von Balthasar and J. Ratzinger, *Mary: The Church at the Source* (San Francisco: 2005).

30. R. Strange, *Newman and the Gospel of Christ* (Oxford: 1981); for the development of Newman's thinking here, see B. J. King, *Newman and the Alexandrian Fathers: Shaping Doctrine in Nineteenth-Century England* (Oxford: 2009).

31. Athanasius, *Contra Arianos* 3, 3.

32. Thomas Aquinas, *Summa theologiae*, Ia., q. 43, a. 5, ad. ii.

33. H. Denzinger, *Enchiridion symbolorum, definitionum et declarationum de rebus fidei et morum* (Freiburg: 1991, 37th edition), pp. 142–43.

34. J. H. Newman, *Tracts Theological and Ecclesiastical* (London: 1874), pp. 204–5.

35. Ibid., pp. 218–19.

36. Athanasius, *De Incarnatione* 20.

37. W. Kasper, "'One of the Trinity . . .': Re-establishing a Spiritual Christology in the Perspective of Trinitarian Theology," in idem., *Theology and Church* (London: 1989), p. 108.

38. In *Vatican Council II: The Basic Sixteen Documents*, trans. Austin Flannery, O. P. (Northport, NY: Costello Publishing Company, 1996).

39. G. Macdonald, *Unspoken Sermons: Series I, II, III* (Radford, VA: 2008), p. 227.

40. Maximus Confessor, *Ad Thalassium* 60.

Chapter 4

1. *Lamentabili*, proposition 25.

2. Vincent of Lerins, *Commonitorium* 23, 3.

3. J. Pereiro, *Ethos and the Oxford Movement: At the Heart of Tractarianism* (Oxford: 2008).

4. H. U. von Balthasar, *Theologik II: Wahrheit Gottes* (Einsiedeln: 1985), pp. 225–55, especially 245–50; note the aphorism from his friend the metaphysician Gottlieb Soehngen, "Metaphysics without metaphor is empty; metaphor without metaphysics is blind," cited at ibid., p. 248, n. 3.

5. Y. Congar, O. P., *The Meaning of Tradition* (San Francisco: [1964] 2004), p. 98.

6. J. N. D. Kelly, *Early Christian Doctrines* (London: 1977, 5th edition), p. 40.

7. H. de Lubac, S. J., *The Splendour of the Church* (London: 1956), p. 15.

8. Hippolytus, *Traditio apostolica* 3.

9. Leo, *Sermo* 5, 11.

10. C. Journet, *The Church of the Word Incarnate: An Essay in Speculative Theology* (London and New York: 1955), I, p. 403.

11. J. H. Newman, *Theological Paper VIII*, 25 February 1866, in J. D. Holmes, ed., *Theological Papers on Inspiration and Infallibility* (Oxford: 1979), p. 110.

12. *Lumen Gentium* 4, citing Cyprian, *De oratione dominica* IV, 23.

13. The phrase in its Christological reference is drawn from Thomas, *Summa theologiae* IIIa., q. 48, a. 2, ad i; the pneumatological development is described in H. Mühlen, *Die Kirche als das Mysterium der Identität des Heiligen Geistes in Christus und den Christen: Eine Person in vielen Personen* (Paderborn: 1967, 2nd edition).

14. J. H. Newman, *Parochial and Plain Sermons*, IV, 11 (London: 1900), p. 174.

15. Congregation for the Doctrine of the Faith, *Communionis notio*, 9.

16. H. de Lubac, S. J., *The Splendour of the Church*, p. 76.

17. Cited from *Institutions liturgiques* by Y. Congar, O. P., *Tradition and Traditions* (New York: 1967), pp. 434–35.

18. J. Corbon, *The Wellspring of Worship* (New York: 1988), p. 95.

19. Y. Congar, O. P., *The Meaning of Tradition*, p. 142.

Chapter 5

1. O. Blanchette, *Maurice Blondel: A Philosophical Life* (Grand Rapids, MI: 2010), p. 81, with an internal citation of M. Blondel, *Action (1893): Essay on a Critique of Life and a Science of Practice* (Notre Dame, IN: 1984), p. 364.

2. J.-H. Nicolas, O. P., "Réactualisation des mystères rédempteurs dans et par les sacraments," *Revue thomiste* LVIII (1958), pp. 20–54.

3. Thomas Aquinas, *Summa theologiae* IIIa., q. 48, a. 2, ad. i.

4. C. Marmion, *Christ in His Mysteries* (Bethesda, MD: 2008), p. 18, with an internal citation of Isa 53:4.

5. H. U. von Balthasar, *Theo-Drama: Theological Dramatic Theory*, vol. 4, *The Action* (San Francisco: 1994), pp. 383–88.

6. J. H. Newman, *Lectures on Justification* (London: [1838] 1874), p. 216.

7. E. Schillebeeckx, O. P., *Christ the Sacrament of Encounter with God* (London: [1965] 1971), pp. 21–47.

8. Thomas Aquinas, *Summa theologiae* IIIa., q. 56, a. 1, ad. iv; q. 2, ad. iv.

9. Ibid., q. 53, a. 1, ad iii.

10. E. Schillebeeckx, O. P., *Christ the Sacrament of Encounter with God*, p. 222; I have, however, modified the schema to make it simultaneously both ecclesial *and* Christological.

11. Julian of Norwich, *Showings* (Long Text), chapter 60.

12. Cyril of Alexandria, *Commentary on the Gospel of St. John* XII, 20, cited in John Paul II, *Ecclesia de Eucharistia*, 14.

13. D. Farrow, *Ascension and Ecclesia: On the Significance of the Doctrine of the Ascension for Ecclesiology and Christian Cosmology* (Edinburgh: 1999), p. 264.

14. M. J. Scheeben, *Die Mysterien des Christentums* (Freiburg: [1865] 1951), ed. J. Höfer, p. 479.

15. I take the concept of mystical tropology from H. de Lubac, S. J., *Exégèse mediévale: les quatre sens de l'Ecriture* (Paris: 1959–64), I/2, pp. 549–620.

16. St. Peter Chrysologus, *Sermo* 117, cited in the Office of Readings for Saturday of the 29th Week *per annum*.

17. T.-M. Hamonic, O. P., "Les fondements de la Morale thomiste," in S.-T. Bonino, O. P., et al., *Thomistes, ou de l'actualité de S. Thomas d'Aquin* (Paris: 2003), p. 171.

18. E. Gilson, *The Spirit of Medieval Philosophy* (London: 1936; Notre Dame, IN: 1991), p. 325.

19. See M. Ouellet, "The Foundations of Christian Ethics according to von Balthasar," *Communio* 17 (1990), pp. 375–401.

20. John Paul II, *Veritatis splendor* 76.

21. Thomas, *Summa theologiae* Ia.IIae, q. 100, a. 9, ad. ii.

22. Ibid., a. 9, corpus.

23. Dante, *Purgatorio*, canto VIII, 88–93. Translation by A. Esolen (New York: 2003), p. 89.

24. For a contemporary exegete's description of New Testament ethics as participation in the Christ pattern of sacrificial love, see L. T. Johnson, *Living Jesus: Learning the Heart of the Gospel* (San Francisco: 1999).

25. Augustine, *De doctrina christiana* I, 36 (40–44).

26. T. S. Eliot, *The Idea of a Christian Society* (London: [1939] 1954), p. 15.

27. Thomas, *Summa theologiae* Ia., q. 59, a. 3.

28. Idem., *Quaestiones disputatae de potentia*, 10, 2, 5.

29. Bread carved with a cross to the accompaniment of the words "Sacrificed is the Lamb of God who takes away the sin of the world, for the life of the world and its salvation."

30. Dante, *Paradiso*, canto XXIII, 73–74. Translation by A. Esolen (New York: 2004), p. 249.

31. M. Schmitz, "An Outline of the Mariology of the Classical Roman Missal," *CIEL Chronicle* (January: 2008), p. 17.

32. *Martyrdom of Polycarp*, 14.

33. J. A. Jungmann, S. J., *The Mass of the Roman Rite* (London: 1959, revised and abbreviated edition), p. 451.

34. J. Siri, *Gethsemane: Reflections on the Contemporary Theological Movement* (Chicago: 1981), pp. 68–69.

35. Cyril of Alexandria, *In Epistolam ad Romanos* V, 18, from among the fragments of his lost commentary.

36. C. S. Lewis, *That Hideous Strength* (London: [1945] 2005), p. 488.

37. Idem., *The Four Loves* (London: [1960] 1998), p. 127.

38. Cited from M. Eliade, *The Sacred and the Profane: The Nature of Religion* (New York: 1959), in S. Caldecott, *Beauty for Truth's Sake: On the Re-enchantment of Education* (Grand Rapids, MI: 2009), p. 128.

39. E. Gilson, *The Spirit of Medieval Philosophy*, p. 280.

40. H. E. Manning, "The Catholic Church and Modern Society," in idem., *Miscellanies* (London: 1877–88), III, p. 312, cited in J. Pereiro, *Cardinal Manning: An Intellectual Biography* (Oxford: 1998), p. 239.

41. Adapted here to the condition of friendship at large are some words used originally to describe the kind of friendship specific to marriage, in S. Caldecott, "Gender as Sign of the Trinitarian Love," *Second Spring* 12 (2010), p. 12.

42. D. Sayers, *Creed or Chaos? And Other Essays in Popular Theology* (London: 1947), p. 43.

43. A. Nichols, O. P., *Hopkins: Theologian's Poet; An Introduction and a Commentary on Selected Poems* (Ann Arbor, MI: 2006); idem., *The Poet as Believer: A Theological Study of Paul Claudel* (Aldershot: 2011).

44. Idem., *Catholic Thought Since the Enlightenment: A Survey* (Leominster: 1998), pp. 139–41.

45. Augustine, *Adversus Judaeos* 10 (15).

46. C. S. Lewis, *The Discarded Image: An Introduction to Medieval and Renaissance Literature* (Cambridge: 1964), p. 176.

47. A. Schwartz, "Theologies of History in G. K. Chesterton's *The Everlasting Man* and in David Jones's *The Anathemata*," *Chesterton Review* XXIII, 1–2 (1997), p. 66.

48. Cited from a letter of 22 August 1963 in R. Hittinger, "The Metahistorical Vision of Christopher Dawson," in P. Cataldo (ed.), *The Dynamic Character of Christian Culture: Essays on Dawsonian Themes* (Lanham, MD: 1984), p. 14; cf. G. K. Chesterton, *The Everlasting Man* (1925), in idem., *Collected Works*, vol. 2 (San Francisco: 1986), p. 248, and D. Jones, *The Anathemata* (London: [1952] 1972), p. 211.

49. Augustine, *In Johannis epistolam* III, 3.

Chapter 6

1. Thomas Aquinas, *Summa theologiae* IIa. IIae., q. 1, a. 7.

2. The contrast between the Triadology of East and West drawn in stark terms by Théodore de Régnon is now considered too sharp; see M. Barnes, "De Régnon Reconsidered," *Augustinian Studies* 26 (1995), pp. 51–79.

3. Gregory Nazianzen, *Oration* 40, 1.

4. *Quicumque* 3–6, in H. Denzinger, *Enchiridion symbolorum, definitionum et declarationum* (Freiburg: 1991, 37th edition), p. 51.

5. J. Meyendorff, *A Study of Gregory Palamas* (London: 1962); C. Yannaras, "The Distinction between Essence and Energies and Its Importance for Theology," *St. Vladimir's Theological Quarterly* XIX (1975), pp. 232–45.

6. J. H. Randall, Jr., *Aristotle* (New York and London: [1960] 1967), pp. 59–69.

7. Compare the suggestion, for instance, that in Aristotle, *Metaphysics* IX, 8, at 1050a 21–23, *energeia* should be translated "is-at-work-ness," in J. Sachs, *Aristotle's Metaphysics: A New Translation* (Santa Fe, NM: 1999).

8. E. Gilson, *The Spirit of Medieval Philosophy* (London: 1936; Notre Dame, IN: 1991), p. 275.

9. I single out here for its lucidity R. Garrigou-Lagrange, O.P., *God, His Existence and His Nature: A Thomistic Solution of Certain Agnostic Antinomies* (East St. Louis, MO: 1934–36).

10. M. Levering, *Scripture and Metaphysics: Aquinas and the Renewal of Trinitarian Theology* (Oxford: 2004), p. 60.

11. Bernard, *In Canticum Canticorum* VIII, 2.

12. Thomas Aquinas, *Summa theologiae* Ia., q. 32, a. 1, ad. iii.

13. Idem., *Scriptum in libros Sententiarum*, I., distinctio 2, q. 1, expositio.

14. K. Foster, O. P., "The Mystery of the Trinity," *Life of the Spirit* XVI. 183 (1961), p. 120.

15. Gregory Nazianzen, *Oration* 31, 14.

16. See G. Emery, O. P., *Trinity in Aquinas* (Ypsilanti, MI: 2003), chapter 5.

17. M.-D. Molinié, *Le Courage d'avoir peur* (Paris: 1979, 4th edition), p. 48.

18. See N. den Bok, *Communicating the Most High: A Systematic Study of Person and Trinity in the Theology of Richard of St. Victor* (Paris: 1999).

19. Thomas Aquinas, *Scriptum in libros Sententiarum* I., distinctio 6, q. 1, a. 2.

20. "Psychological Trinitarian theory [of the Augustinian-Thomist kind] is not a conclusion that can be demonstrated but a hypothesis that squares with divine revelation without excluding the possibility of alternative hypotheses." B. Lonergan, S. J., *Verbum: Word and Idea in Aquinas*, ed. F. E. Crowe and R. M. Doran (Toronto: 1997), p. 204.

21. See R. Bauckham, *Jesus and the Eyewitnesses: The Gospels as Eyewitness Testimony* (Grand Rapids, MI: 2006), p. 6: "In the case of one of the Gospels, that of John, I conclude, very unfashionably, that an eye-witness wrote it"; the full argument is set out on pp. 358–471. While for Bauckham the "beloved disciple" of the Fourth Gospel is not the apostle John but the "John the Elder" mentioned in Papias's *Exposition of the Logia of the Lord*, he draws attention to Dom John Chapman's *John*

the Presbyter and the Fourth Gospel (Oxford: Clarendon, 1911) as the "best case for identifying the two Johns in this passage of Papias" (Bauckham, *Jesus and the Eyewitnesses*, p. 17).

22. Thomas Aquinas, *Super Joannem* 19, lectio 3, no. 2414.

23. Julian of Norwich, *Showings* (Long Text), chap. 4.

24. H. U. von Balthasar, *Theo-Drama: Theological Dramatic Theory*, vol. 4, *The Action* (San Francisco: 1994), pp. 330–32; he takes up a brief account of Bulgakov on pp. 313–14.

25. S. B. Bulgakov, *Agnets Bozhii* (Paris: 1933), p. 121.

26. H. U. von Balthasar, "Abschied von Gustav Siewerth," *Hochland* 56 (1963), 182–84, reprinted in P. Reichenberg and A. van Hooff, eds., *Gott für die Welt: Henri de Lubac, Gustav Siewerth and Hans Urs von Balthasar in ihren Grundanliegen* (Mainz: 2001), pp. 285–88.

27. Augustine, *In Joannem homiliae* 105, 3.

28. Idem., *Sermo* 71, 20, 33.

29. R. Cessario, O. P., *The Godly Image: Christ and Salvation in Catholic Thought from Anselm to Aquinas* (Petersham, MA: 1990), p. 205.

30. W. Hill, O. P., *The Three-Personed God: The Trinity as a Mystery of Salvation* (Washington, DC: [1982] 1988), p. 58; with regard to Augustine, *De Trinitate* VII, 10, no. 4; VIII, 10, no. 12.

31. W. Hill, O. P., *The Three-Personed God*, p. 59.

32. Thomas Aquinas, *Summa theologiae* Ia., q. 43, a. 5, ad. ii, citing Augustine, *De Trinitate* IX, 10. Translation by Fathers of the English Dominican Province (London: 1937), p. 202.

33. Thomas Aquinas, *Summa theologiae* Ia., q. 43, a. 7.

34. C. S. Lewis, *Miracles* (New York: 1947), p. 134.

35. Congregation for Institutes of Consecrated Life and for Societies of Apostolic Life, *Verbi Sponsa* 4: "Their life is a foreshadowing of the goal towards which the entire community of the Church journeys, in order to live for ever as the Bride of the Lamb."

36. Thomas Aquinas, *Scriptum in libros Sententiarum*, I., distinctio 14, q. 2, a. 2.

37. H. U. von Balthasar, "L'Esprit, l'inconnu au-delà du Verbe," *Lumière et vie* 67 (1964), p. 122.